FRENCH
DEMOCRACY

FRENCH DEMOCRACY

Valéry Giscard d'Estaing

With a Preface to the American edition
TRANSLATED BY VINCENT CRONIN

DOUBLEDAY & COMPANY, INC.
GARDEN CITY, NEW YORK
1977

DEMOCRATIE FRANÇAISE by Valéry Giscard d'Estaing,
© 1976 Librairie Arthème Fayard.

ISBN: 0-385-13078-3
Library of Congress Catalog Card Number 76–58100

Translation Copyright © 1977 by William Collins
Sons & Co Ltd and Doubleday & Company, Inc.
Preface Copyright © 1977 by Doubleday & Company, Inc.

For *Marianne*
and for *Gavroche*

Contents

	Preface	ix

PART I FRANCE AS IT IS

Chapter 1 Diagnosis — 3
Chapter 2 The Limitations of Traditional Ideologies — 15

PART II MAN AND SOCIETY

Chapter 3 Unity Through Justice — 25
Chapter 4 A Community of Free and Responsible Men — 39
Chapter 5 A Society of Communication and Participation — 49

PART III THAT FREEDOMS MAY LIVE

Chapter 6 Pluralism and Freedom — 59
Chapter 7 Private Property and Freedom — 69

PART IV THE ORGANIZATION OF POWER IN FRENCH DEMOCRACY

Chapter 8 The Management of the Economy and of Social Development — 75
Chapter 9 The New Growth — 85
Chapter 10 Freedom, Order, and Security — 93
Chapter 11 A Strong and Peaceful Democracy — 101
Chapter 12 French Democracy in the World — 113

CONCLUSION AN AMBITION FOR FRANCE — 119

Preface

The history of democracy in France has been a constant source of amazement to American observers. Here they see a country whose theoreticians, from Montesquieu to Tocqueville, have clearly expounded the principles of democracy, a country which experienced the greatest political revolution of modern times. Yet in the nineteenth century this same country founded a European empire for the first time in a thousand years, restored the old Capetian line to the throne, saw two predominantly proletarian revolutions, and set up a bourgeois republic.

In his fascinating "Recollections," Alexis de Tocqueville, the author of *Democracy in America*, has given us a lively though rather melancholy account (remarkable for its keen understanding of the behavior of crowds and feeling for odd situations) of his part in the Revolution of 1848. It left him heartsick and disillusioned, and he devoted the last ten years of his life to pondering the reasons why the Revolution had failed. At the time of his death in Cannes the Second Empire was at its height.

* * *

The main reason for the malfunction of democratic institutions in nineteenth-century France was that no one was willing to accept democracy as a permanent set of rules, incumbent upon all, upon pressure groups as well as individuals. Each individual or group regarded it as a means of attaining specific results, held to be essential at a given time. Thus democratic suffrage was used, quite justifiably, as a means of introducing equality of political rights and, later, of bringing about a reduction in social inequalities, more to the advantage of the petty bourgeoisie who, thanks to their numbers, were replacing the old privileged classes, than of the proletariat.

On the other hand, the rules of democracy were accepted only when they favored the needs and aspirations of the moment. France made use of democracy as an instrument but was reluctant to accept its constraints.

* * *

This is hardly surprising.

No other Western country has lived as long as France under so highly centralized and hierarchical a system of government.

In its heyday this system did France the great service of making it the most unified and best governed country in Europe. At a time when Germany was disintegrating into a jumble of petty principalities, when England was torn by bloody dynastic rivalries, France, under the rule of a single family, was unifying its administration and army, and carrying on a foreign policy worthy of the most populous and powerful country in Europe.

The reverse of the coin was a monolithic centralized authority, from whose decisions there was no appeal. Our national psychology still bears the mark of this excessive centralization. It explains why over a long period of time democracy was regarded in France not as a theory of government, but as a means of winning power. And once gained, this power was once again wielded in accordance with the same old centralized, hierarchical system, which seemed to have become the real constitution of France.

*   *   *

The times have changed.

Advances in education, living standards, and communications, combined with the increase in population, confront France with new problems. *French Democracy* offers an attempt at a solution.

Various solutions might have seemed possible. An American sitting down to write a book on "Democracy in Europe" might, for example, suggest a radical decentralization of France, leading to an internal federalism similar to that which the victor powers imposed on West Germany in 1945.

First of all, this would be going counter to the immense effort at unification which France pursued for centuries and which was the basis for its success. One might as well ask China to plan its cultural disintegration. Moreover, such a suggestion fails to take account of an essential factor in our present political thinking: the striving for a European confederation. Favoring, as it does, a confederated Europe, France cannot afford to atomize its internal structure. The national unity, which was the source of France's strength from the fifteenth century to the Empire, must be preserved if France is to play an advantageous part in a European confederation.

*   *   *

The new French democracy will be oriented toward pluralism: Political pluralism, implying a diversity of parties and institutions. Economic pluralism, signifying a rejection of monopolies and of state capitalism as well as state socialism. Cultural pluralism, which stands for tolerance, diversified media of opinion and information, and for freedom of creation, expression, and research.

To my way of thinking, pluralism is the conception in which political freedom, economic spontaneity, social aspirations, and cultural emancipation converge. Thus I am convinced that the new French democracy must be a pluralist democracy.

* * *

I do not know how many American readers will be interested in this message. Historical developments, geography, and differences in our ways of life and modes of communication have led to a certain estrangement between our two countries in spite of all they have in common, especially their passion for democracy.

I am not unaware of the prejudices and irritations that divide us, but I am no less aware of the ties of friendship that unite us.

In the present book I aspire to contribute an idea to the development of democracy, the idea of pluralism extended to all social life. I dedicate my idea to Alexis de Tocqueville, my brother in intention if not in talent, who never ceased to wonder why men persisted in looking to revolution for what could be obtained without violence, without hatred and tragedy, by the exercise of reason and good will.

FRENCH
DEMOCRACY

Part I

FRANCE AS IT IS

CHAPTER 1

Diagnosis

French people today find it difficult to understand the society in which they live. The speed of the changes it has undergone, the contradictory nature of the results of these changes, and the powerlessness of traditional ideologies to provide completely satisfying guidelines account for this perplexity.

Our national characteristics compound the difficulty. Many Frenchmen are convinced that they would prefer living in a peaceful, rustic, and familiar world, similar to that of the past, but economically and socially transformed, while at the same time they resent the changes this requires. They want a familiar society but a new improved model. But they find this new improved model difficult to define, and are in consequence not just uneasy but deeply anxious. They fear the future more than they like it.

* * *

If we look at what has been happening to French society, we find that before the war, and even in the early fifties, France showed every sign of being both advanced and traditional. Advanced because of the high standard of its intellectual life, the inventiveness of its art, the variety and talent of its political life, its contribution, unfortu-

nately a declining one, to the progress of science. Traditional because it was rural and thrifty, masculine and ruled
by the elderly, centralized and hierarchical.

In the France of that period the gulfs between social
groups were immense, much wider than in comparable
countries such as the United States and Germany. Now
and again children from the state schools made their mark,
but that did not conceal the compartmental nature of the
society. The classes were sharply differentiated by standard
of living, by food, dress, and housing, even by thought and
language. Prewar films show clearly the contrast between
the *grand bourgeois*, the *petit bourgeois*, the worker and
the peasant. Everything conspired to separate the social
classes, so that passing from one to another was a difficult
feat, rarely achieved.

That society may have possessed truly liberal political
structures, but it placed powerful constraints on the individual. The great social institutions—family, school,
Church, and of course state—imposed their authority without sharing it, even if they did so good-naturedly.

In twenty-five years a sort of hurricane has struck this
quiet world. A revolution more powerful than any political
revolution has taken place at the heart of French society,
affecting all its structures: family, school, university,
Church, moral code. It has been caused by a combination
of three factors: unprecedented economic growth, the massive spread of education, and the permanent eruption of
the audio-visual media into everyone's life.

Between 1950 and 1975, that is in twenty-five years,
hardly time enough for sons born during the war to become fathers, the national product more than tripled in
volume, and real consumption per head of the population
nearly tripled; the infant mortality rate was reduced by 25
per cent; a man's life expectancy increased by six years

and a woman's by eight. The amount spent on food declined by half, that spent on hygiene and health increased threefold. Six times as many young people obtained their baccalaureates. The minimum old-age pension increased fourfold in real terms. Eight and a half million houses or apartments were built. Twenty-five years ago no one had a washing machine or television set; in 1975 seven out of ten households had the former, nine out of ten the latter. In 1953 a car was owned by 8 per cent of workers, 32 per cent of the middle-income bracket, and 56 per cent of the higher-income bracket. In 1972 the figures were 66 per cent of workers, 86 per cent of the middle-income bracket, 87 per cent of the higher-income bracket.

Things change so quickly that words cannot keep pace. There are today half the number of peasants there were in 1950, but if we take the word "peasant" in the sense it had twenty-five years ago there are no peasants at all. The peasant has become a cultivator of land, a qualified factor in the economy. He has changed much as the wheat he grows has changed. The strains in use today differ more from the strains grown immediately after the war than those did from the ones grown three centuries ago. There is more mechanization on farms today than there used to be in industry. It is hardly surprising if the farm worker's way of thinking, living, and behaving have little in common with their equivalents twenty-five years ago. What is true of the agricultural worker, a symbol of stability, is true of every profession and every activity. Words have remained the same, but the country has not. It has changed more since 1950 than it changed in the eighty years before 1950.

The extent of that evolution has been partially concealed by political circumstances. First of all, it happened in a period of exceptional political stability. Our institutions were established in 1958 and 1962 at the prompting of General de Gaulle and, after having been violently opposed by part of the body politic, are no longer really challenged. The French people feel what they have seldom felt in the past: that on the whole they possess a political system adapted to the running of a modern state.

Secondly, the very stability of the political system and therefore of the men in office, who of course had simply been voted in, has given an impression of immutability, whereas in fact the country has been shaken to its foundations. The upheaval took place without the trumpet calls of political revolutions, behind people's backs, as it were, and this explains the difficulty they have in measuring and defining it.

The French character, however, has remained the same. It is quick to the point of being volatile, instinctively generous but held back by an earthy possessiveness; eager to discuss but sometimes preferring the *fait accompli*; fervently proud of France but poorly informed about what foreigners think of their country; full of all sorts of ideas, but conservative about immediate surroundings; witty, discerning, decent, but fond of easy jokes, feasting, and arguing. The French pretend to be cynical and they like boasting, but all things considered they are the world's most sensitive people. The democracy designed for France must take account of these elements in the French character, of the intelligence of Gavroche and the smiling kindness of Marianne.

* * *

The result of this evolution is first and foremost immense progress. Like happiness for individuals and peace for nations, progress is the thing we notice least, so I should like to remind the reader of certain facts. I would ask him to set aside his prejudices and the current feeling of gloom, and to consider their full significance.

There has been national progress. France has ceased to be an archaeological, gastronomic curiosity and become a modern, respected nation. It is the world's third largest exporter, on a par with Japan, and it has a gross national product 56 per cent higher than Britain's, thereby taking the lead in Europe's oldest competition. It is equipped with the tools for efficient production. As a result of these advances, it has a wider freedom of action abroad.

France's material and social progress is seen in the tripling of the workers' purchasing power in twenty-five years. If that change seems to us inevitable, let us remember that its very possibility was doubted a few years ago; indeed, in the fifties the Communist Maurice Thorez was still upholding the theory that workers are doomed to total penury.

It is difficult for us to appreciate this evolution because of the fall in the purchasing power of money, but it is a fact beyond dispute. It becomes obvious if we look at the real price of goods, that is, the amount of work necessary to buy them. In twenty years, from 1956 to 1976, the prices of food products, in terms of hourly wages, have fallen from 100 to 55; and those of manufactured goods from 100 to 41.5. In order to earn what they need to buy the same goods, French people have to work half as long as twenty years ago.

Eloquent though they are, these figures give only an approximate idea of how the gap between different patterns of life has narrowed. For when incomes rise as a whole, even if differentials are not reduced, different lifestyles tend to become more similar in food, clothes, holidays, and even, to a lesser degree, housing. Beyond a certain point, as we see in the United States or in Scandinavia, the same additional income brings with it a smaller social differentiation.

Again, the massive increase in the media means that the whole population receives the same daily news and every evening watches the same shows, that is, shares the same culture. Whether that is good or not so good is another question, to which I shall return, but the point is that for the first time since our prehistory, it is the same culture.

Finally, there has been progress for the individual. The history of French society is the history of the individual's thousand-year-old effort to increase and assert his autonomy. Never before, unless perhaps in the very first years of the French Revolution, has so much important ground been covered so fast.

The emancipation of women in material terms and before the law, even if not yet complete, has in the last two years reached a point that places us in this respect at the head of the world's nations. The emancipation of young people has recently been given a legal basis. No previous generation even began to possess such opportunities for choices. Individual freedom is ceasing to be an abstract right and becoming a real fact of daily life.

When considered objectively these results prove the capacity of our type of society to initiate and absorb change. They ought to have led to a near-unanimous confidence in that society. But while this progress has been taking place, a whole new range of problems, those raised by growth and those which growth has not solved, have arisen to block our road. They remind us that man's progress is not linear, and does not lead to one definite point on the horizon. It is more like the biological drive of nature, which every year obliges man to clear the ground of weeds and undergrowth, to sow and to create order, as though nothing had ever been achieved.

* * *

These problems, new or as yet unresolved, are of three kinds: Some concern the relations between social groups; others the individual's place in society; the last, connected with the birth rate, concern society itself.

The everyday working of our social organization, which governs the relations between the social groups within it, still falls short of the truly just society we would like to live in.

Objective studies show that economic growth has markedly reduced the inequalities in society, and those who are not convinced by the statistics have only to read Zola or Maupassant's peasant stories. Nevertheless, growth has not altogether eliminated inequalities and has sometimes created new ones.

Past inequalities which still persist despite recent growth affect women, especially in their professional life, and they affect certain poor areas of our country, either the land itself or industry. They affect too the opportunities open to children, and are all the more unjust for being often cumulative: Handicaps resulting from insufficient income, from a broken home, from inadequate educational facilities, often pile up on one and the same person.

As for the new inequalities, it looks as though they are actually fostered by economic growth. At one end of the chain we have the so-called excluded: that is, those who cannot do productive work and so have long been excluded from the redistribution of wealth. In this group are many old people; and, owing to the complexity of the administrative machinery, they are sometimes deprived of the social help intended for them. At the other end are those who make no real contribution to the collective effort toward growth, but have taken up a well-chosen position, as robbers used to lie in wait for merchants at a bridgehead or on a stretch of road, in order to extort exorbitant sums or advantages from other people's work.

The second group of problems arises from the difficult relations between the individual and society.

Economic growth has made possible the real emancipation of the individual from the restraints which used to oppress him and the unavoidable misfortunes which made him wretched. But it has been accompanied by the individual's closer dependence on society as a whole, something that everyone feels and either wants to speed up or to reject altogether.

He is dependent on the consumer society. Basic activities that used to be mainly done by the individual or by his family, such as cooking meals, traveling, amusements, have been transferred to the business system. Examples range from food and clothing to the organization of holidays, by way of beauty care and the management of savings. The result is a higher quality of goods and services available to consumers, but on the debit side the individual is increasingly dependent on the services and goods furnished by the economy.

He is dependent on the collective services of society: The increase in such services of every kind, notably in the fields of health, education, and transport, provides the individual, his family, and his children with ever more plentiful goods, forms of security, and advantages. On the debit side the individual is increasingly dependent on an administrative system over which he has scarcely any control and to which he feels himself handed over, bound hand and foot.

When he goes out to work, he is dependent on the system of production. Industrial firms, and now business firms too, have become vast and impersonal, and division of labor is carried to extremes. In his daily life he is dependent on great urban developments: overcrowded towns and huge soulless blocks of flats.

Paradoxically this increased dependence on society is accompanied by a reduced participation in society. The small community of former years, where everyone knew everyone else, and which enmeshed the individual from the cradle to the grave, in a network of ceremonies, attachments, and loyalties, has been superseded by a host of more diffuse relationships. This growth has made it possible for the individual to enlarge his horizons and has given him more freedom. But it has also made social integration more fragile and more tenuous.

The weakening of neighborhood ties, the partitioning of social groups, the specialization of space and time in modern life, all lead to a kind of fragmented world, where the fabric of human relations is split, where loneliness and anonymity reign, and where each individual in his outsize pile of concrete and glass longs for a lost unity.

These fundamental facts, which cannot be dissociated from the technical and economic change of our time, lie at the root of the most obvious evils and feelings of unease in our society, which are brought to light, disseminated, and magnified by the media, until they are known to us all. Despite the rapid improvement of the general standard of living, we find demands by this or that group becoming angrier. We have what would seem to be a paradox in a rich society: inflation. It stems from stiff competition between groups and categories for a share in the nation's resources, and also reflects the difficulties we as a nation find in choosing between demands that exceed the present capacity of our economy. We find a new violence, apparent not only in delinquency and maladjustment but, more deeply, in the strident language used by each social group, in the excesses and intolerance of the proposals of certain of their spokesmen, in the latent temptation to resort to force. Lastly, and this is the most worrying of all, because it affects the living cells of society, we have the moral confusion of many of our fellow citizens.

To cap all this, a world economic crisis, the most widespread and severe since that of the thirties, has temporarily deprived us of the two benefits which, after twenty-five years, we had come to believe we would always enjoy: full employment and a continuous rise in the standard of living.

The third problem which deeply affects society is the disturbing change in our birth rate.

For centuries France was the most populous country of Europe, but at the end of the nineteenth and the beginning of the twentieth centuries its birth rate went through a long period of stagnation. France was the only nation to experience this in a world of rapidly increasing population.

Then, after the war, the birth rate shot up. That stimulated the nation's development. Not only did it lead to the growth of our economy, but it gave France back its vitality, its ability to change, and the dynamism of a young country.

Suddenly, from 1965 onward, in all the industrialized countries of Europe and North America as well as in the Soviet Union, the birth rate stopped rising. France was the last country to experience it, and so far to a lesser degree than other countries. But we have not escaped the trend. The birth rate is no longer sufficient to maintain our present population.

This phenomenon is unusual in that it affects many countries at the same time, and despite current research scientists have not yet been able to explain it.

But this is a problem we have to face. It is obviously in the interests of the country as a whole that the birth rate should again rise steadily. But it is also in the interests of every Frenchman if we intend to continue making progress and to strengthen solidarity between the different generations.

* * *

So much for our progress and for our problems.

To come to terms with the former and to solve the latter, the French people feel the need of a total explanation. They want an over-all plan. Instinctively they turn to familiar ideologies, only to discover that these are powerless to help.

CHAPTER 2

The Limitations of Traditional Ideologies

The task of ideologies is to provide explanations that make it possible to analyze reality in order to guide action. The traditional ideologies, Marxism and classical liberalism, no longer fulfill the first condition. How then can we expect them to fulfill the second function?

These two systems of thought have opposed each other for more than a hundred years, a surprisingly long time by modern standards. In other fields of knowledge or research, for example in physics, chemistry, and biology, the theories of the nineteenth century have been several times revised and modified, such an approach being considered an excellent example of scientific activity.

Classical liberalism and Marxism for the most part lie outside the field of science, so it is passion more than reason that has kept them alive, although they are less and less representative of observable facts in our societies, less and less adapted to the solution of our concrete difficulties. It would be interesting to discover why, when everything else is changing, human thought has clung so long to these two abstract models, each of which is manifestly partial though revealing a part of the truth. The answer is doubtless that they represent a quasi-religious form of compensation at a time when faith in traditional religions has dwindled.

I do not intend to discuss these two models in any systematic fashion, because that has been done a hundred times already. The partisans of one have shown forcefully and pertinently the inadequacies of the other. These heterocritical studies fill whole library shelves. In any other field scientific method would have obliged us to abandon these imperfect theories and to look for a new, more satisfying model. But political passions, private interests, and fixed opinions darken our judgment to the point where the two champions remain proudly encamped, face to face in the middle of the political arena, their armor corroded by rust.

Marxism and classical liberalism are inadequate theories, because they oversimplify the facts and, still worse, misunderstand the nature of man.

* * *

Marxism has contributed its share of the truth. In contrast to the nineteenth century's ideological concept of "bourgeois conquerors" and thanks to its founder's admirable analytic method, it was in its time a demystifying and investigative force.

By revealing the reality of class structure behind the fiction of a unity composed of individuals reputedly equal but in fact equal only before the law, by disclosing the underlying links between social institutions and structures of production, by demanding real rights as opposed to the purely formal aspects of freedom, Marxism has helped the industrial societies of Western Europe to analyze themselves better, and their working class to obtain legitimate but long unrecognized rights.

But in the hands of the faithful, and in the absence of

any all-embracing representation of man, it has become in its turn a means of mystification. Marxism mystifies when it claims scientific status while ignoring the disciplines of science; when it attributes all oppression to economic power; when it reduces the history of nations to the class war; when it confers on one particular class a messianic and redemptive role.

Of course Marxism has appeared to evolve. Concepts such as capitalism's fatal and definitive crisis, revolution springing from the working classes of the most industrialized countries, the proletariat's rise from total to relative poverty and to the dictatorship of our own day, were once put forward as integral parts of Marxist doctrine, but have been successively forgotten or abandoned—sometimes discreetly, sometimes with maximum publicity—as it became necessary to mask the most obvious contradictions between doctrine and reality, or at any rate the least acceptable discrepancies between Marxist morality and morality pure and simple.

It is a fact, however, that in France, unlike other countries, Marxism still plays an important role in intellectual and political life, and there are several reasons for this. First, the social sciences in France are insufficiently developed, and opinion about the facts is constantly preferred to knowledge of the facts themselves. Another reason is the instinctive appeal to minds brought up in the Catholic tradition of a total explanation, of a monorationalism in place of monotheism. Similarly, the emphasis on the class war, which lies at the heart of Marxism, links up with that taste for total opposition, for the negation of others' existence, and the refusal to compromise which are an inheritance from Gallic individualism and the fierce ardor of the Frankish tribes, and thus in the continuing tradition of French politics.

But this is not the whole story. We have apparently

come to equate perception of the fundamental evils of our society—injustice and privilege—with the worth of the doctrine that has most clearly denounced them. The equation is perhaps a false one, for it confuses acuteness of perception with the logical value of a system, but insofar as the equation is made emotionally, it is both persistent and respectable.

Ideology is sometimes ahead of the facts, but in this case it lags behind. It might be compared to an outgrown garment constricting a developing body. Marxism no longer helps us to understand the new elements in our society; it is certainly no guide to building that of tomorrow.

* * *

Classical liberalism also fails to provide us with a key that opens all doors, although we owe it a debt for having helped us to achieve social progress. First and foremost it has upheld our political freedoms. Because it places the individual at the beginning and end of social organization, classical liberalism is the foundation of political democracy in its most perfect form. The French clearly recognize this fact; indeed they do not imagine democracy in any other form. That is why, in our country, even the theories most opposed to freedom must dignify themselves with its feathers; hence some very queer birds.

We also owe liberalism a debt for providing us with the basis for our economic achievements. After twenty-five years of peaceful rivalry, the free enterprise system, involving competition at home and abroad and the smooth working of market forces, has been proved superior in two respects to authoritarian planning, even when such planning is termed "democratic." First, it allows production to be determined directly by individual needs instead of handing over to a bureaucracy the job of deciding what those needs are. Secondly, it uses initiative as a psychological and technical mainspring, instead of relying on clumsy administrative decisions.

Nevertheless, classical liberalism does not take account of contemporary social reality.

It invites us to consider economic life as a vast arena in which individuals equal in all their rights freely confront one another. From there it goes on to postulate that the actions of the individual under the stimulus of competition will be those best calculated to promote the general good.

Experience does not contradict these claims. Competition, by obliging every man to give of his best, is certainly the most effective known stimulus. But experience also shows that, just as an animal defends its territory, so the natural reaction of men is to ensure their own safety by exercising their ingenuity to build up defenses against competition.

Consequently so-called liberal society has seen the development of codes and guarantees, various protective systems, coalitions and agreements, unions and federations of employers, of which the ultimate effect, though claimed to be in society's interests, is to restrict competition. Faced by such concentrations of power and the phenomena of domination and withdrawal that they provoke, state intervention becomes, in the last analysis, not a threat to freedom but the true guarantee of the freedom of the weakest.

Although it has been markedly evident in our societies over the past decades, classical liberalism is unaware of this change.

Likewise, classical liberalism takes only a partial view of human nature and therefore of man's aspirations. It has been said a hundred times that *Homo oeconomicus*, that one-dimensional robot who acts only according to his material interests in the narrowest sense, is useful when we have to introduce a pseudo-human parameter into mathematical equations, but actual man engaged in economic and social life cannot be reduced to a single component.

Just as the citizen taking part in political life is more than a Sleeping Beauty waking every five or seven years to cast or abstain from casting his vote, so man, as an individual and as a member of society, has many dimensions. He has fears and passions, he has a will to power and a desire for justice, he is capable of sacrifice and solidarity, he longs for friendship and human warmth, he wishes to serve his family's needs, he has cultural aspirations and ideological convictions.

Classical liberalism, too, throws only a partial light on the needs of our fellow citizens, of man in the round with all his contradictions, desiring both security and adventure, material comfort and humanism, freedom and order. The more our society progresses, the further man diverges from the crude liberal robot.

What we need is a different analysis and a different plan.

* * *

Plainly neither of the two great social theories of the nineteenth century takes full account of the change in our societies since the theories were formulated and therefore of the reality of our social life today. This is not surprising, for life cannot be enclosed in a system, and the one thing the two theories have in common is an abstract, partial view of man.

Doubtless that was inevitable when the theories were conceived. The harsh realities of industrialization and the class struggle were bound to focus attention on economic restraints and the functioning of the means of production.

But the two models have furthered our knowledge. They provide two useful, even necessary, stratifications in our society's accumulated self-knowledge. But we have seen the message of both dry up as they become detached from the real world. It is necessary to move on further, to plan and to build.

Before attempting to do so, I shall define my starting point, the point from which the eye seeks, and finds, a perspective. For everything depends on what one is looking at and the point from which one is looking.

The two models I have been discussing are "systems" constructed by taking as a starting point the consideration of over-all mechanisms found in the economy, from which are drawn conclusions that refer the argument back to man.

The progress of knowledge today makes possible a different approach. We can start our argument with man and his needs, and from there go on to choose the best mechanisms.

This "anthropocentric" approach is based on two principles:

1. Creative activity lies at the source of economic development. Economic organization must be conceived as a deployment of man's creative activity.

2. Man has the political and social capacity to speak out, repeatedly and in specific terms, about the organization of the society in which he intends to live. That society must therefore be a society of responsibilities, expressing, at various levels, the capacity of the individual to take part in defining his social world.

It is a question, to some extent, of superimposing consciousness on spontaneity, and of realizing a synthesis between the development of individual liberties at the human level and the rational organization of collective functions.

The most modern approach will be not the one that starts from the analysis of the economic mechanism, but the one inspired by man's need.

It will be the French approach. It leads to the pluralist society.

Part II

MAN AND
SOCIETY

Any plan for society is defined by the place it accords man and by the relationship it establishes between the individual and the collectivity.

But individuals are not atoms floating in a void. They form groups, communities, and social classes. What must their respective positions be; what proportion of space is reserved for them in society? On this question depend many others, so it must be examined first.

Three approaches commend themselves:

Instead of letting itself be split into sections or groups that either dominate or are dominated, our society must strive to create its unity by means of justice.

It will constitute a community of free and responsible men.

It will be a society of communication and participation.

CHAPTER 3

Unity Through Justice

A united society is the necessary end result of the long evolution of the Christian West. It began around the eleventh century with the appearance in the early towns of a category of men who were neither nobles nor peasants. The evolution was continued at the Renaissance; in the eighteenth century, guided by the *philosophes*, it became general, and then irreversible when the division of society into social classes ceased to be considered as the inevitable consequence of a divine plan.

Our society will not be completely reconciled with itself until the old divisions have been removed.

That does not mean that our society is dedicated to leveling and uniformity. Nor does the abolition of social classes mean that roles and jobs must be made uniform.

It does imply, however, that differences between jobs should not inevitably continue unchanged from one generation to the next, so that privileges and handicaps are handed on automatically.

Further, it means that differences between individual jobs which produce an inequality of effort, talent, risk, and responsibility should not be such that individuals have the feeling of belonging to different worlds; on the contrary, they ought all to feel members of the same community. In any given society there exists "a maximum social divergence" in the rewards accorded activities and talents; it varies according to the social climate, and beyond that maximum the social fabric tears.

It is obvious that French society still has a long way to go before reaching this goal of unity. What we have to decide is how best to get there.

*　　*　　*

The experience of collectivist societies shows that they have failed in this respect.

According to the central tenet of their philosophy, collectivization of the means of production ought to end any possibility of a division of society into classes. But despite the paucity of scientific studies of themselves which such societies provide, enough is available for us to see that the theory has not worked in practice.

Take two examples: on the one hand the hard lot of the peasants (that is, of the most numerous class), and on the other, except probably in China, the privileges enjoyed by party members of those in positions of power, and transmitted from father to son—these are class phenomena. The head of a powerful collectivist country declared about ten years ago that 70 per cent of the students at the university he was visiting were students because of their parents' status.

*　　*　　*

Is a more unified society a utopia? Not at all. The gradual ending of class differences is one of the fundamental results of the historical evolution of Western-style societies. Like all structural phenomena, this is the more evident the longer the period under review. It is impossible to observe on a yearly scale; it becomes perceptible in the middle term; and in the long term it is undeniable. Recalling social relationships at the end of the nineteenth or at the beginning of the twentieth century, even in a country with a republican tradition like ours, we are at once aware of the distance covered.

It is true that our progress has been too slow, but it has been in the right direction. Compared with the relative failure of collectivist experiments, it demonstrates that a conscious process of evolution can bring about the unification in depth of society.

This claim seems contradicted by the frequent antagonisms of the French people. But we must not deceive ourselves: The divisions are more ideological than sociological, and they do not correspond to class divisions. That is shown by all the available evidence. If certain political leaders, in face of the facts, struggle to demonstrate that class distinctions are worsening rather than improving, they are turning their backs on reality and everyone knows it.

The fact is that France is socially on the road to unification, under the impulse of three factors which we must constantly bear in mind: the rise in the standard of living, education, and the widespread dissemination of news.

The evolution now taking place, far from leading to a confrontation between two classes—bourgeois and proletariat, strongly contrasted and antagonist—is characterized by a large expanding amorphous central group; its exceptionally fast numerical growth, its links with both categories of society, its capacity to absorb from both, and the modern values it stands for, place this central group in the position of gradually and peacefully absorbing into itself the whole of French society.

On one side, through its technicians, foremen, skilled workers, and certain independent workers, it borders on the industrial proletariat. On the other side, through its managers and other independent workers, it borders on the bourgeoisie. It is not itself a proletariat; that is, a mass of men with no protection, cut off socially and culturally from the rest of society. Nor is it a bourgeoisie; that is, a clear-cut social group defined by the exclusive possession of an economic and cultural heritage. It is a social reality of a new type, mobile and open to change, expressing values borrowed partly from the proletariat, partly from the bourgeoisie, and which, when linked, are those of a modern society. Hard-working but farsighted, ambitious but capable of generosity, numerous but individualistic, it really resembles nothing except itself. And, I should add, it is typically French in its characteristics and way of life.

This central group is not a product of theorists' imagination and is not put forward here for the convenience of argument. It exists, it is alive, we meet it daily.

Contrary to certain glib assertions, France is not divided in two over major social problems. The spectrum of opinion is much wider and more finely gradated than that. If one had to trace lines of cleavage on the majority of important issues, none would go down the middle. Our country's sociological center already possesses real unity and the figures suggest that it comprises much more than half the population.

Its vocation therefore is not to be recruited as reinforcements for battles with which it is not concerned, whether a delaying action by those who wish to prevent social change or an attack launched by prophets of the proletariat's messianic role. Its vocation is not to be made use of by others, but itself gradually to transform French society by absorbing into itself a society from which divisions are progressively removed. It can do this because the values it embodies are already shared to a large degree by the majority of our society.

Thus—and this is the essential point—the unification

of our society does not imply a dramatic break with its past evolution, but an accentuation of that evolution.

To attain this objective, there is no question of going back on the current trend. The various aspects of progress achieved up to now have not all been spontaneous, of course. The conscious action of men and the play of social forces at work in an advanced industrialized country can, by helping each other along, move the country forward on the road to unification.

* * *

A conscious human collectivity must manage its own evolution. The men of our day are in a position to guide our society's advance toward a more complete unity.

The measures for speeding up this evolution are necessarily very different in kind and scope. Here we are not concerned with their details, but to determine their goal and define their spirit.

Two simple words suffice to express them: justice and solidarity.

The specific content of the demand for justice and the extent of the solidarity are not the same in every age. The role of elected representatives and of the public powers is to express and to accomplish, in each period, what the collective conscience terms justice.

Today, if we go beyond doctrinaire theories, we find that most people are convinced that justice consists in the elimination of poverty, in the disappearance of privileges, and in the struggle against discrimination.

Poverty is the lot of every society that has appeared on our planet. Ours is one of the first to have had the privilege of being able to eliminate it, just as smallpox and the plague have been eliminated. It would be unpardonable not to give priority to tackling this task and not to solve its problems with all speed.

Poverty degrades. Like racism, it affronts human dignity. Old age, unemployment, the early loss of a spouse, personal handicap—no such event or situation can justify a prosperous society abandoning one of its members to the distress of poverty.

To fight it one can choose a general method or particular actions. The general method would be to guarantee every Frenchman without exception a minimum income. If his own resources do not reach the minimum, society makes up the difference.

This radical method has the virtue of simplicity. But people are not ready yet for so profound a change, which would place a heavy burden on society. We can only try it out. So it is going to be done for one category of persons: widows and women living alone with a child in their care.

In other cases, specific means of action have been chosen. Very important measures have been taken to help old people benefiting from the "minimum old-age pension," handicapped adults, and workers laid off for economic reasons.

This work will be continued and systematized, especially for the old, in order to give all Frenchwomen and all Frenchmen the certainty of an income that ensures they shall have a dignified old age, and to provide them with a ready means of obtaining it. In short, we must free the French people from the anguish of a penniless old age. Financially speaking, the task already accomplished and the task remaining are very onerous, but they must be seen in perspective. They will eliminate poverty by a network of measures; they will ensure each member of society, whatever his age or difficulties, a minimum income, so that he remains a full partner in society.

Justice is also the ending of privilege. The French had

a revolution to accomplish that. But human nature is such that privilege never completely disappears. Eternal vigilance and a strong will are necessary to prevent its reappearance.

Whatever demagogues may say, ending privilege does not mean leveling, or preventing people from achieving outstanding success. We accept as just the sudden success of certain artists, great barristers or doctors, certain businessmen—I wish there were more of them—certain scientists and intellectuals doing exceptional creative work. Such people are rare and their work is carried on under precarious conditions.

But justice does not permit a man to grow rich unless he has worked for his riches, or has talent, nor does it permit some of the most favored to escape their share of taxation. We must therefore eliminate three basic kinds of privilege: monopoly, chicanery, and tax evasion.

The temptation to monopolize and to escape competition is found everywhere, both among the self-employed and among certain wage earners. Every monopoly defends itself tooth and nail by evoking grand principles and vested interests. Whenever possible, it parades a shoal of "small fry," in order to divert attention from a few big sharks. But every monopoly is a potential abuse. The collectivity must fight and eliminate them, and to do so it needs the support of public opinion.

Nor is it acceptable that a few individuals, by devious operations and trickery, should grab the fruits of a collective effort to which they have not contributed. Property speculators are the prime example. The law which has just been passed takes a new approach and covers the full extent of this problem; in built-up areas it gives back to the collectivity what the collectivity has worked for. It is a just law, which will be applied with the utmost care.

The privilege of tax evasion is also unacceptable. Each

person must contribute to public expenditure according to his capacity. The scrupulous taxpayer feels an increasing rebelliousness at the thought of the person who, legally or not, escapes taxation.

That is why the taxation of capital gains is an act of justice. All advanced foreign countries have such a tax, and it was laid before the Assemblies and made law in order that justice should be done. It must be applied straightforwardly, with that purpose in mind.

Justice too demands that we step up the fight against tax fraud. Naturally the individual's democratic rights must be respected, and he must be given guarantees similar to those he enjoys in the law courts.

This task will end only when French people are convinced that all are equal before the revenue authorities, just as they are where other public duties are concerned. Twenty years ago public opinion viewed the ending of tax fraud with irony, ten years ago with skepticism, but now it supports and approves what is being done.

Finally, our society must know how to recognize and fight discrimination. I shall give four examples to illustrate how necessary and how difficult that is.

The first and in my view essential task in this field is to improve the position of women. For thousands of years their subordinate position has seemed, even to women themselves, the result of a decree of nature. Today this discrimination has less and less economic or ideological justification, and would seem to be purely and simply an injustice. A true democracy must fight to eliminate it in as many ways as the discrimination is exercised, in all walks of family, professional, and political life.

The mental and social resistance blocking any improvement in women's status will have to be overcome so that men and women enjoy complete equality, though this does not necessarily imply that they will have exactly the same roles.

Women will be the first, but not the only ones, to benefit. I am convinced that their special aptitudes, their distinctive way of seeing the world and of acting on it will make a fundamental contribution to the development of our society. The ending of those discriminations that still weigh on women is doubtless a matter of justice, but not only of justice. It is, rather, a decisive element in our general social evolution. It will help our society to eliminate violence more completely, while at the same time giving realities precedence over ideologies. In short it will help our society to advance to a new stage of human awareness.

The completion of the task of allowing women to play a full political and social role in the community is a permanent objective for our society. This development, which affects half the population, is likely to enrich our social life more than many reforms affecting only the other half.

I often think of the immense potential in terms of sensibility, imagination, and realism which such feminine participation will allow our society to draw on. For two years France has been one of the most progressive countries in the world in this field, and the task of integrating women into social life will be carried out in full.

Manual workers, at least a great many of them, also suffer from obvious discrimination. It is apparent even at school, in the distinction which many teachers and families arbitrarily draw between general education and technical education. It is apparent in professional life, in wage levels that reflect neither the responsibilities nor the arduous nature of the work; in inadequate security; and in the fact that the professional life of most manual workers, as opposed to other groups of wage earners, has no career structure.

This characteristic is not found to the same extent in

Germany or Britain. It is probably in part the result of our old Latin culture and of the violent and unjust reactions against the working class after the Revolution of 1848 and the Commune of 1871.

The discrimination cannot be justified on social grounds, any more than discrimination in the other direction could be. Production in a complex modern business results from collaboration. Each individual, manual worker or not, plays an equally indispensable and worthwhile part. Discrimination handicaps us because it keeps part of the active population from jobs created by our industrial development. Indeed it is a structural factor in underemployment. If we are to be economically efficient and to secure social justice, we must fight discrimination.

We should also consider the people who are sometimes called "nonactive," though that term reveals the prejudices that weigh upon them.

Because they do not take part in paid productive work, or because they have retired, they have hardly any means of making their voice heard. The active members of society, wage earners and others, inevitably take their share first.

Society's conscience has an important responsibility here. Justice must be done to the nonactive, by ensuring them adequate resources. As a matter of urgency we must increase pensions. We must also increase the loans available to women with young children or large families and make them simpler to obtain. The necessary funds will be found.

This program is indispensable, but by itself it is not enough.

Social life itself is often organized as a direct function of the needs and aspirations of active people. It is therefore a form of fighting injustice when we see to it that town planning and leisure activities, housing funds, the expenditure of public moneys, and even the vocabulary we use respect the dignity, rights, and interests of families and old people.

The most intolerable discrimination is the one directed against certain children.

That people possess varying degrees of talent and courage is a fact, and it is only common justice to admit it. But justice must also ensure that, whatever their background, our children can develop and find in their social life the equal opportunities they deserve.

A democracy which is sincere must give priority to this objective, while recognizing that much patience and immense efforts will be required to achieve it. One method alone or one action in isolation are not enough to compensate children for handicaps resulting from inadequate family life or some other misfortune. An over-all approach is necessary.

Education of course plays an essential part. Socially, the schools must do more than ensure that society reproduces itself identically; they must help to create greater equality.

The establishment of a single system of secondary schools for all young French people will play a powerful part in ensuring equality of cultural attainment. We must follow that up by defining in school curricula a "basic knowledge," which will vary with the times and as the civilization it expresses develops.

Schooling alone cannot bring about equality where life has created inequality. Hence the importance of a "second chance," in the shape of further education. The development of such facilities, available to all, is one of the concrete conditions of a real democracy. Finally the diversity of means of access to the different professions, the manifold channels to promotion, even the organization of social life, all must tend toward giving everyone an equal opportunity.

I will give a small but significant example. The establishment of the National School of Administration has met the desire to unify and democratize the senior civil service. Compared to the prewar situation, it is an obvious success. But it has been found that the most gifted students come from backgrounds close to the senior civil service, and for that reason those who apply to enter the school and pass the entrance exams come mainly from Paris. The result is that Parisians make up an increasingly large proportion of the student body, and the area of recruitment has tended to narrow. We must think up new admission schemes: in short, go back to the drawing board.

Justice demands ending of poverty and privilege and discrimination.

These constitute our first but not our only task. We must try to work out how large a differential between jobs is socially justified at a given period in a given society.

It is obvious that some differentials are necessary to reward hard work, talent, risk, and responsibility. To deny that would not bring us any nearer justice.

But how can we determine the desirable range of what I have called "the maximum social divergence"? That is a difficult question to which there is no objective, unanimous answer, no answer that is valid once and for all. But it remains an essential question, once we realize that when they reach a certain scale, these differentials become "desocializing"; they destroy the individual's sense of belonging to the community.

The answer is not to be found in ideological theories or doctrinaire concepts, but in watchful, progressive practice, as for example in the policy of "contracts," which has worked well in the public sector.

Year after year open-minded employers and responsible trade unions have negotiated wage settlements for all levels of the work force. Discussions of necessity have been tough, but every time agreement has been reached about how wage increases should be apportioned.

During the last two years, though they were made more difficult by the economic crisis, agreements were generally based on a decision to give priority to increasing the lowest wages, instead of, as formerly, increasing wages proportionately. At the same time the necessary action has been taken to prevent the hierarchy of wage groups from collapsing.

Such agreements are possible only between partners who do not refuse compromise on principle, who prefer to seek agreement rather than misunderstanding, who decline to subordinate social action to political aims. That is another matter, to which I shall return.

The important thing to realize is that the fair division of increased profits can be decided in common as the result of a sincere dialogue between partners of good faith.

Such an evolution is possible, and must take the form of carefully thought out, concerted action.

* * *

Some people are going to ask whether it is really necessary to raise all these questions. After all, society has always accepted a certain measure of injustice. Does it not weaken society and uselessly embitter it to list its imperfections, when these are in the nature of things?

They are wrong. First because their realism is only apparent: In French society today only a minority adopt an attitude of resignation. The less favored young people and those with a strong sense of responsibility will not accept privilege or discrimination. French society cannot resign itself to imperfection when its deepest forces call for improvement.

Others are going to say: You admit the system is bad; therefore it must be overthrown.

They too are wrong. A social system is not bad because it openly and lucidly admits certain of its failures and begins to put them right, any more than a sick man is a candidate for euthanasia because he goes to his doctor. A social system is condemned only when it hides its weaknesses and refuses to put them right, or if it exaggerates their extent and sinks into morbid contemplation of them.

Another attitude is possible, and it alone is worthy of a democratic society: to measure objectively what is not just and to take the necessary corrective measures without either procrastination or precipitation.

In this way, striving hard for more homogeneity, guided by the will to end poverty and privilege, to fight discrimination, to reduce excessive inequalities in living conditions, and to ensure equality of opportunities, our society will pursue its path toward unity by way of justice.

Here, I suggest, is the source of a new momentum which will do more than the timid measures of conservatism or the clashes of revolution to make the French people warmer and more fraternal.

CHAPTER 4

A Community of Free and Responsible Men

Our society is based on the fulfillment of the individual.

The countries of the third world are hardly in a position to choose their goal. They are bound to think and act in terms of the masses. To feed, clothe, educate, and house the masses is their first task and it leaves little room for consideration of the individual. We must bear that in mind if we are to judge some of their policies fairly.

French democratic society must also take account of the general needs of the collectivity, but at the same time it is able to turn toward the fulfillment of the individual.

At the stage of economic evolution we have reached, our objective is to promote the development of every single personality, to allow each individual to be master of his life. This responds to the deep longing of French people and what is most characteristic in our national culture: an appreciation of the value of the individual and the taste for freedom.

A collectivist concept of social organization, dominated by the idea of mass, is at the opposite pole from the evolution our society desires. Here we come to the heart of the matter. It is not enough to put a coat of paint, even red, white, and blue paint, on a collectivist plan to make it suitable for French temperament and needs. No social plan is valid for France unless it aims at giving a wider, more vital freedom to each individual.

I am thinking of course of the fundamental freedoms which the French nation won for itself. Some people make themselves ridiculous by calling on us to strive for, and secure, those freedoms, forgetting that we already possess them, indeed that we are one of the very few countries in the modern world to do so.

I am thinking also of more modest freedoms, each of them incompatible with a collectivist theory of society: freedoms in private life; freedoms in professional life.

In private life freedom implies access to a home resembling as little as possible a cell in a cement hive and as much as possible a house; whenever feasible, it should belong to the family. It implies the right to choose freely one's doctor and lawyer; to decide what one's children will learn and where one will spend a holiday. . . .

In these different fields powerful organizations, some profit-making, others not, have been formed: friendly societies, offices for social housing, company projects or projects run by company committees, travel organizations. They provide irreplaceable services and are one of the achievements of our age, as long as they serve the individual. But as soon as they impose on the individual, legally or illegally, he is no longer freed but dependent. So we must be careful that none of them ever acquires exorbitant power.

That amounts to saying that the collectivist organization of daily life would be a regression for our society. It is curious how some people praise that system as found in other countries, whereas ironically enough their way of life clearly indicates that they themselves would not submit to it for a moment.

Society's task is not to regiment the individual in order to condition his mind, but to free him, so that he may fulfill himself.

Now that more of men's material needs are beginning to be satisfied, their cultural aspirations are going to become increasingly important.

In contrast to collectivist societies, our society has chosen freedom of expression and creation, limited only by the need to protect the public's feelings. We must find more ways for everyone to share in our cultural heritage, and for the individual to use all the instruments of culture, so that he may express to the full his curiosity, sensibility, and creative powers.

In professional life society should be so organized as to promote the fulfillment rather than the stultification of personality. Education must be intelligently planned and of a high standard, so that those leaving school are able to choose their profession. There must be more security and better working conditions, more of those experiments—so far rather timid—to enrich work and to organize self-contained teams of workers. There must be further education, affording a second chance, not so much to rectify a youthful mistake as to afford opportunity for promotion. Finally, salaried workers must have more opportunity of becoming self-employed, since this offers more freedom and responsibility.

Such a concept of professional life is at the opposite pole from collectivism. This is obvious in the case of the self-employed. Say a farmer, artisan, or shopkeeper sets up on his own. If we treat his action not as a relic of a bygone age but as a valid form of self-advancement, we are arguing against collectivism, for that system has been proved hopelessly inefficient in agriculture, craftsmanship, and business.

The same holds true of the wage earner. Under whatever political regime, technical necessity has led to the formation of large industrial and business firms in certain sectors of the economy, and these imply the existence of powerful collective structures representing management and workers. If individual development is to be encouraged, it must not be throttled by these structures. The worker must be free to choose the firm he works for and to leave it in order to join another, without getting anyone's permission. No system or administration should control the employment or promotion of workers.

More generally, the cure for the pressures on the individual in modern industrial life is not the collectivist remedy of still more organization, and therefore still more pressure. It is rather the protection and development of all the workers' individual liberties.

* * *

Our society is based on the responsibility of the individual.

Security is not a mania for safety, but the erecting everywhere of a safety net, that is, of minimum guarantees that are as high as possible, and above which the individual's initiative and responsibility have full play.

In our lifetime we have seen the rapid growth of institutions aimed at protecting everyone against the chief risks of life: sickness, unemployment, and old age. Such a development is a positive gain. One of the injustices of society in the old days was to make the individual pay for the consequences of events or situations over which he had no control.

This security and protection against the unavoidable must be still further improved and extended, along the lines of the programs already mentioned. The final aim is to protect every Frenchman from poverty. For two years now workers made redundant by economic circumstances have been entitled to 90 per cent of their wages, and this represents a further progressive step by society. Likewise, the extension of social security to the whole French people, which will come into force on January 1, 1978, will crown fifty years of development. It meets a real need.

But in a society directed toward man's fulfillment there has to be a limit to collective responsibility. The abuses practiced in certain cases of unemployment benefit and in the working of the sickness benefit are only two examples which show that a line has to be drawn somewhere. Just as it is right to guarantee people against events over which they have no control, so it is pernicious to exempt them from playing their part where they are able to do so, without turning for help to the collectivity.

A number of people loudly proclaim themselves in favor of the autonomy of the individual, but at every turn demand more guarantees from the collectivity. They are careful not to specify the cost. They probably count on the public being naïve enough to believe that any increased aid will be free, or paid for exclusively by others.

How far that is from the truth is shown by the facts of life today. Even if we exclude income tax, each of us pays around 35 per cent of his earnings for the various kinds of security we enjoy. If this percentage were to rise still higher, everyone would probably get less, not more. The question is whether the percentage of an individual's earnings over which he has no jurisdiction should increase indefinitely. Or should we—as I believe—protect the individual and his freedom to choose by setting a limit, beyond which we would get a different kind of society?

Even more important than these financial considerations are those aspects of the problem that concern personal responsibility and the right to take the initiative.

One of man's strongest motives is the need to assert and surpass himself. It lies behind his greatest achievements, and his deepest joys. That is why, far from discouraging initiative and diluting responsibility, the democratic society encourages these qualities.

Collectivist systems do not neglect this side of human nature, which is unalterable, but they take steps to tame it to their own advantage. Starting from the principle that the mass is superior to the individual, they canalize individual energies by varying doses of collective emotion, propaganda, and group enrollment along the lines laid down by the central power.

These systems are not inefficient but they are only suited to simple tasks. Every army in the world appeals to the collectivist instinct in order to mobilize its soldiers' energy. The same instinct can galvanize large numbers of men for major public works or land programs, but the more complex the production, the less likely is a collectivist organization to be effective. This is why it is noticeable that as economy and society become more advanced the collective principle enters into ever-increasing contradiction with the state governing the forces of production.

Collectivist societies have less and less grip on individuals and cannot arouse initiative or responsibility, so they fall victim to inertia and inefficiency; hence the slowness of their growth, their trade deficit, and all the characteristic signs of inflation.

But more is at stake than social efficiency. We must not forget what takes place in the minds and hearts of individuals.

It would be unjust not to recognize the joy a human being feels at belonging to a group. But to offer the way of unison as the sole means of fulfillment is to mutilate men's souls. Once the festive lights have gone out, a gray sadness grips collectivist societies.

Human beings reject the life of the ant colony. As the world's cultures show, they are seeking diversity. They have the feeling of truly growing in dignity and of experiencing joy to capacity only when they exercise full responsibility in every aspect of private and professional life. That is why there is no place for collectivism in our democratic society.

The taste for assuming responsibilities and the capacity for exercising them are not things we are born with. They are developed by education and apprenticeship; they atrophy when they are not used and when we let things slide.

The abundance of consumer goods in a rich society, the guarantees furnished by our security systems, the spiritless obedience demanded by large organizations, the passivity of the individual solicited by advertising and the mass media; all these things weaken individual initiative and have led to a widespread bitter resignation, usually termed "unease."

On the other hand, the raising of educational standards, the variety of factual information available, the increase in the number of choices offered us at every moment, must make people more enterprising in their private and professional lives.

Our democratic society will strive to develop in its members the taste and capacity for being responsible and will provide them with the means.

We must re-examine from that point of view the following aspects of collective life: education in the family, at school, and for a job or profession, work itself and the possibilities of promotion, the functioning of social security systems, and the organization of daily life.

This is a path that has been little explored, but it will be of decisive importance in the progress of our society.

* * *

To face a world where the pace of change makes him dizzy, to make his contribution to society and receive from it what it can give him, man today needs every available chance and all his strength. Two examples, the family and education, will illustrate this.

Family life is one of the conditions of the individual's fulfillment.

For the collectivist society, preoccupied above all with its hold on the individual, the family is a potential rival, and therefore an object of mistrust. Even if it does not always go so far as deliberately to set children against their parents, such a society takes care to keep the family in a subordinate role.

Classical liberal thought has no place for such ideas and accords the family at least legal autonomy. But it treats the family as something private. If it so happens that the existing conditions of social life are opposed to the fulfillment of the family, too bad; and it is not surprising if the families of the less well off were made painfully aware of this.

In a truly humanist view of society, on the contrary, the family must be upheld for its own sake and allowed full participation in social life. We should aim at fulfillment of the individual, not cramping of individual freedom, as those who hanker after a patriarchal society would wish. Like certain related species, man is so made that he needs family intimacy in order to express his feelings fully and to achieve balance.

There is no need to call family life in question in order to improve it. Such improvements would include the equality of husband and wife within the family circle, the recognition that each child has its own personality, and respect for its autonomy.

Since the family is indispensable to human happiness and growth, since it is invaluable to adapting the texture of society, we must take care to shelter it as far as possible from vicissitudes and dangers, both collective and private. We shall apply an over-all policy whereby families are given the means to take their place in social life and, whenever necessary, to mold the organization of society to their needs.

Man must also be our starting point when planning the great work of education and training.

Education and training, whether in school or in daily life, should aim at ensuring that every person has as much autonomy as possible, and at developing his personality and his capacities. From this flow three consequences.

First, equality must be the rule. Every kind of teaching must be free, and special care must be given to those whose social background places them at a disadvantage. The basis of the curriculum should be the same across the country, and one aspect of this principle, as I have mentioned it, is that all young French people now go to the same type of secondary school.

While seeking to promote personal autonomy, education and training must also strive to give each individual the best weapons for life in the world. They should develop his general knowledge and give him adequate professional training, so that he is really master of his job or trade, instead of being its slave. Education must also develop his critical spirit and his personal judgment, so that he understands the influences acting upon him, instead of submitting to them passively. Nothing would be more opposed to the aim of education in a pluralist society than to indoctrinate young people with an ideology.

Lastly, education must develop the imagination no

less than sensibility and intelligence, manual ingenuity no less than the power to reason abstractly. It must think in terms of individuals, adapting itself as far as possible to the personality and gifts of each pupil or student. In other words, it should help them to find their place in society.

CHAPTER 5

A Society of Communication and Participation

Our society must be one of communication and participation. To suggest that the men and women of our country should pursue their individual interests in selfish isolation would be to ignore the deepest aspirations of French society today, especially those of the young.

Hence the need to go further in two respects.

We must go beyond quantity to quality: from the standard of living to the kind of life we are leading, from payment for work to the content and the meaning of work, from random growth to a new kind of growth; from the destruction of nature to ecology.

We must go beyond ourselves to others, so that, by expressing and exchanging opinions and by full participation in the community, we may re-establish the communication which our society of reinforced concrete and administrative form-filling has lost. It is a matter not of indirect communication, organized on a massive scale, but rather of person-to-person communication, building up a true community of individuals.

To re-establish communication in society, which has been temporarily blocked by the size and facelessness of contemporary projects, will be a major task.

This leads us to consider four areas where we must boldly change course. They are town planning, the reform of the civil service, the evolution of industry, and the role of associations.

* * *

The first change of course requires a new conception of the town.

Among the great achievements of the Fifth Republic is the building of 7.5 million homes, which ended the dramatic shortage brought about by thirty years of rent freeze and government inertia.

Many of the new housing estates, however, are a source of grave dissatisfaction. With a few deserving exceptions, the buildings of the last twenty years were inadequately planned. We have built, or allowed construction companies to build, housing complexes which are monotonous, out of proportion, and collectivist in spirit. Such places give rise to violence and loneliness.

Today we must give priority to homeowning rather than renting, to individual dwellings rather than a collective block, to improving the old rather than building new, to the small town rather than the big city, and call a halt to the spread of the idea that bigger is better.

In this way we will create a framework for living scaled to the individual, respecting what is already there, favorable to a personal life-style, fostering communication and a neighborly spirit.

* * *

A change of direction is also required in public administration.

We are fortunate, it is true, in possessing a competent and honest civil service, and this is a rare benefit. But it must be admitted that its relations with the public are far from perfect. There is too much paper work, misunderstanding, anonymity, bureaucracy. In spite of itself, our civil service sometimes provides a taste of what a collectivist society would be like. It was developed, in fact, to carry out certain clearly defined tasks with supreme authority, whereas social change has made it one of the principal partners in our daily lives.

It must change. It must deal with people face to face, treat the person administered as a fellow citizen, reinvent a language people can easily understand, solve problems rather than pile up new documents, realize the value of time. This is a fascinating task for new generations of civil servants, because it means creating a new kind of language and mode of action.

* * *

Much has been said about modern man's alienation from his work. The crushing size of certain firms, the weight of hierarchies, and the division of labor give the worker a feeling that he does not belong to himself and is a stranger to his work.

As a remedy, some people have advocated workers' control, whereby "the workers' collective" appoints and controls the directors of the firm, which has previously been nationalized.

We should note first that workers' control does not really live up to its name, which suggests that the worker in industry has regained control of his work, whereas in fact it does not end hierarchy or specialization, which are the main causes why workers in large firms often feel they are passive cogs in an anonymous machine.

Secondly, we find that it is in the nature of every firm to incorporate various contributory efforts: work of all kinds, particularly skilled management, savings invested or loaned, raw materials drawn from the environment or provided by society as a whole. The firm cannot be identified exclusively with any one of these aspects, however important. Again, the running of a large modern firm is usually far removed from the function of capital or labor. It is the job of salaried management, and it is up to management to make the various partners in the firm work together.

Furthermore, because of the mass of technical, financial, and commercial methods which they have built up, large firms, whether liberal or collectivist, are necessarily institutions. Their horizons, both in space and time, are much wider than those of any one of their employees. Their aims therefore cannot be the same. The long-term needs of the production belt and the immediate interest of the workers, which is to obtain the highest wages, cannot, objectively speaking, coincide.

That is why, in every society where they are free to do so, the workers have created their own organizations, such as trade unions, workers' delegates and committees, in order to express their own interests, which are different from those of the firm.

The converse is also true. If that is misunderstood, there is too often a danger of subordinating the present to the future in the running of a business.

Lastly, the task of a modern firm is to co-ordinate with great precision and accuracy a considerable number of activities, interests, and energies, all different in kind. This day-to-day achievement is possible only if the great number of movements involved is directed by an authority, and if the principle of that authority is not continually being called in question. With attitudes as they are today, it is inconceivable that this condition should be fulfilled in firms where the appointment and control of directors are subject to permanent struggles of a political nature.

That is why in an industrial society workers' control in the strict sense can be only a temporary phase or a mere semblance. No economy or people can long support the disorders and impotence which inevitably stem from workers' control. Unless the machinery of a liberal economy is reintroduced, the central power in one form or another has to take matters in hand. The few known experiments in workers' control show that it is only a schoolbook hypothesis. Workers' control is not a stable system. Is it doing workers a service to try to lead them in that direction?

The manifest impossibility of applying workers' control in large firms may lead its partisans to try it out in small ones, which implies first taking the firm away from its owner. So the idea of workers' control leads to a general collectivization of the economy.

Here I imagine you will be struck with despondency.

It is terrifying to think that the hazards of politics might lead France to such a situation. France prides itself on being one of the most intelligent countries in the world, but it has a hard time competing with efficiently organized countries, some organized on liberal lines, others with a social-democratic structure, and none of them prepared to consider workers' control. France would find itself outclassed for a long time because of the resulting disorganization of its economy. It would soon reject an inapplicable method, but only after tasting its bitter fruits.

The reform of the inner organization and working of business must be sought in two ways.

On the one hand, participation of workers' representatives in the life of the firm, so long as it does not impede the exercise of responsibilities, fulfills the workers' desire to be involved in decisions that concern them. This participation is particularly meaningful at executive level, because executives have been trained for it by nature of their functions. In the first instance the law must make possible this participation by defining how it would work and entrusting the firm and those involved with the task of putting it into practice.

On the other hand, progress must be sought at the level of the workers themselves, for their chief desire is to organize their jobs.

If business is to be reformed, all those working in a firm will have to put their shoulders to the wheel. The structure of the hierarchy will have to be simplified by removing wherever possible unnecessary grades. Experiments will have to be made with self-contained teams and the individual worker periodically given the opportunity to voice his views on the nature and conditions of his work.

Without losing their productive efficiency, industry, business, and administration, in which so many French people spend the greatest part of their lives, must gradually become a true human community, allowing of initiative, responsibility, and communication.

*   *   *

To promote communication within society, an important place must be given, lastly, to the development of associations.

The association differs from the mass organization. The latter has its ideology, language, and strategy. It is a power playing power politics with its own members and with the world around it. The association is a group of men and women gathered together for a common purpose which they achieve themselves, without intermediary or pressure, and one which is often in the public interest.

The association is an essential means of action and expression in a democratic society.

* * *

Finally, what are we aiming at? By way of associations we are trying to rediscover man in the city, in the civil service, in business and industry, and to re-create communities of men and women. Our aim is not to enclose the individual in a network of restraints, as in rural society of the old days, nor, as in a collectivist society, to annihilate man in a mass which is itself subject to manipulation. Our aim is to restore to the individual the dimension of fraternity, with its warmth and loyalties.

A society of free and responsible men then becomes a community.

Part III

THAT FREEDOMS MAY LIVE

Implicit in all our thinking about society is our thinking about power.

A society of democratic freedoms necessitates a pluralist structure of power. But this pluralism cannot be purely political: It must be total.

We shall now work out the consequences.

CHAPTER 6

Pluralism and Freedom

We have indicated that liberal thought is inadequate, and also that it is very much of the moment. Classical liberalism is inadequate because it recognizes only political power, whereas power is also economic, social, and spiritual, and it is of the moment because the liberal concept of a plurality of powers flourishes, whereas on several continents collectivist systems are failing to bring about the democratic exercise of power.

In France those who have carelessly derided liberal thought for sixty years now pay tribute to it, though the praise is rather forced. The suddenness of such a swing and the ease with which it happened cast doubts on its genuineness. But the intellectual change it implies has for that very reason even more significance.

In our part of the world today the only admissible concept of power is a liberal one. Let us take note of that.

But ideas require to be thought through thoroughly. If a pluralist structure of power is compatible with democracy, why should this hold true only in politics? That would presuppose that politics is entirely independent of other activities, a mistake which Marx was one of the first to point out.

Pluralism is indivisible. It extends to the whole of society and affects every aspect of it. Pluralism throughout society implies that the various powers at work in our societies can in no circumstances intermingle, least of all the following four: the power of the state, economic power, the power of mass organizations, and the power of mass communications. This is a modern application of the old rule about the need to separate power.

Parodying a famous phrase, we can say that every society in which these powers are not separated fails to respect pluralism.

A truly democratic society must be wholly pluralist. This requirement holds good for each of the above-mentioned powers taken individually.

* * *

The pluralist structure of political power naturally implies a party system and the freedoms that go with it, but also an effective division between them and the powers of the state. The Constitution of the Fifth Republic provides that the executive shall be independent of the legislature, a principle which the majority party has respected. Our republican tradition provides that the judiciary shall be independent, and that its independence shall be guaranteed by the President of the Republic. I have been scrupulous in protecting it.

It implies also that communes and regions must have real power.

We are burdened with centuries of centralization. They have brought about the overdevelopment of Paris and the underdevelopment of certain provinces, as well as the proliferation of regulations and the insufficient development of responsibilities.

It is against the liberal principle of power to discuss at the top questions which can be solved at the bottom. A powerful movement of decentralization is necessary, transferring decisions from Paris to local bodies with more power and appropriate funds.

Let there be no misunderstanding. It is not enough to tinker as in recent years. We must aim at an essential change in relations between the state, local bodies, and the citizen.

Of course we must avoid upheaval in such matters. We must set ourselves a realistic objective, acceptable to public opinion, and work toward it. That is why a high-level planning body has been set up, to work out the optimum structure for local government at the end of the twentieth century, and to restore to local bodies their functions, their responsibilities, and adequate funds. A fundamental law will have to be passed laying down the proper duties of the state, of the *département*, and of the commune.

In Paris the hundred-year-old special administration has been ended and the city enjoys the usual government by elected representatives. This is an example of change in local affairs achieving its goal. Democratic society has given Paris a mayor.

At a higher level of local government it will be necessary to change the respective powers of *département* and region, because three local bodies are too many at a time when alignments within Europe are beginning to occur. This must be done in the next few years, after the present regional institutions have been given a full and fair trial.

Important though this question is, it deals only with the manner of decentralization, whereas the essential point is the principle of decentralization, which must be applied boldly.

* * *

The need for plurality in mass organizations is now generally and officially admitted, notably by all the political parties. Whether this agreement is sincere is another matter, but agreement there is.

* * *

Pluralism is essential also for mass communications.

First, pluralism in the press, which it is indispensable to safeguard, and which justifies a state subsidy to offset the printing charges of newspapers. A commission on which all the interested parties are represented should consider ways and means of preserving the variety and independence of newspapers.

Secondly, pluralism of audio-visual communications. The splitting of the former authority for radio and television into several national bodies mutually independent has helped to guarantee our liberties. Independence and competition must be encouraged at every level, and the quality of programs maintained.

* * *

In these fields the need for pluralism is not denied, at least not openly. In economic affairs the situation is very different.

For several years the question of the nationalization of major French industries has been the center of political debate.

Here too the pluralism of powers is indispensable: If we were to make an increase in the number of nationalized industries, so that all major undertakings were directed in government hands, it would weaken democracy more than it would strengthen it.

The foreword to the Constitution of 1946, to which the present Constitution makes reference, foresees the nationalization of industries when they are public services or monopolies. This concept governed most of the nationalization at the time of the Liberation. It has never been called in question. Recently it led the government to propose the nationalization of electricity in Martinique, Guadeloupe, Guiana, and Réunion, omitted from the law passed in 1945.

But far from being a panacea, nationalization must be envisaged only as a last resort, for increasing the number of nationalized industries inevitably leads to an alarming concentration of economic power, and then of power itself.

It is true that a nationalization which allows competition to continue, like that of Renault in 1945, does not substantially modify the structure of economic power. It does scarcely more than change the procedure for appointing directors.

On the other hand, it obliges the taxpayer to pay for compensation (except of course when a firm is confiscated) and to put up any new capital required.

Experience shows, moreover, that nationalized industries in competition with private firms make little profit and pay only a small amount of corporation tax. So nationalization alters the pattern of taxation by increasing the amount payable by the taxpayer and firms in private hands.

Such, in sum, are the changes that have taken place.

But these changes are precisely those criticized by advocates of collectivism: The nationalizations they demand are quite different from the nationalization of Renault. Their aim is to withdraw industries from competition and to subject them to "democratic," i.e., authoritarian, planning.

Their argument has a certain logic. What is the good of increasing the number of nationalized industries if no changes are made in the structure of economic power and the principles on which industry is run?

We see from this that keeping a firm's capital in private hands is not a curious anachronism, a detail depending on the social system of the day. On the contrary, it is inherent in a certain organization of the economy, entailing competition and industrial autonomy. It is impossible to have one without the other, as we see when we turn to a map of the world and look at the distribution of each system. No country in which the majority of the industries have been nationalized enjoys the freedoms we insist on in France.

This means that the systematic nationalization of industry necessarily implies the choice of a profoundly different economic system, in which firms are no longer autonomous, and where competition gives way to centralized organization.

Such a system brings grave inconveniences at the economic level. But, worse, it contradicts the democratic principle of the plurality of powers.

When major industries, by virtue of being nationalized and subject to authoritarian planning, are directly controlled by the state and its bureaucracy, a society ceases to be pluralist. The power in it is so concentrated that it is bound to be oppressive.

If economic power coincides with the power of the state, who will protect us from economic power?

The concentration of power, notably that which arises from the fusion of political and economic power, leads away from democracy, not toward it.

Systematic nationalization is in no way necessary.

What is the goal, or at least the openly admitted goal, of those who advocate nationalization? It is to withdraw activities important to the country as a whole from the abusive influence of excessively powerful private interests, in particular from monopolies or great financial organizations.

But the means for doing this already exist and owe nothing to collectivization. They are: competition, counterweights, and public control.

Competition is the best weapon against monopoly and market domination. It fights them by dislocating the systems they have constructed.

Thanks to its wise decision to join the Common Market, France has for fifteen years been open to foreign competition, which has played an irreplaceable part in our economic progress, and is an important weapon against monopoly in areas of sophisticated technology.

In certain sectors the size and power of the large multinational combines are such that there is not enough competition, even on a world scale. To remedy this, international action will be necessary and here the European Community has an important role to play. Appropriate action on a national scale is also indispensable, and this justifies what has been done in France in key sectors.

Equally necessary is a policy of competition at home and a struggle against cartels and groupings aimed at dominating a market.

Competition does not just happen. The state has to intervene to establish and maintain it, in face of our national tendency toward tacit agreements. In the past few years the state has had to take legal action against large firms, and such action will be continued. The prevention of monopoly is essential to a democratic way of economic life.

Side by side with competition go counterweights.

A vigorous trade union movement, independent of industrial enterprises, of the state, and of political parties, constitutes a powerful and essential counterweight, as we see at home and abroad every day.

Consumer organizations, which are just beginning to be formed, are a second counterweight.

Every economic system in which workers and consumers do not possess autonomous organization fails to be fully democratic. Nationalization cannot take the place of these counterweights.

Finally, control by the collectivity itself is indispensable. The collectivity must define the responsibilities of every important economic power and make them respected.

Sometimes it will have to defend the interests and rights of consumers and workers, of those who lend money or of small shareholders, of suppliers and subcontractors; at other times it must defend the environment; but always, working within the law, the collectivity must protect against the abuses toward which every powerful firm, public or private, inevitably tends. An important part of our legislation is aimed at this, but clearly it must be increased and improved.

In order that control should be real and protection adequate, the controller (that is to say, the collectivity) and the controlled (that is to say, the firm) must be kept separate.

So nationalization is not necessary in order to protect society from domination by economic forces. And if it allows the state to dominate society, it is positively dangerous.

Instead of collectivizing the capital of large firms, capital investment must be spread through the country as a whole.

In industrial democracies small and medium-sized firms are usually family firms, whereas bigger firms are in a very large number of hands; hence they do not possess the same measure of control as they had in the classic period of industrial capitalism. Only the joint effort of a large number of people makes it possible to raise the capital needed by large firms. In the most advanced countries, therefore, capital for industry comes from an increasingly wide sector of the population.

This is happening in France, though less than in countries which were industrialized earlier. The state must go on devising ways for small savers to invest in their country's industry, to set definite goals, and to see that they are achieved.

*   *   *

So we see what a true democracy entails. It does not consist in capping a centralized social system with an apparently pluralist political superstructure. On the contrary, it implies extending pluralism in depth to the whole substance of society.

Such a change does not happen of itself. The task before us is to develop pluralism and what it entails in political, economic, and social life.

CHAPTER 7

Private Property and Freedom

One of the conditions of freedom is a certain degree of security.

A tramp walking the highways can be described as free. But to the tramp his freedom feels more like a cruel fate.

To be able to enjoy his freedom in security, a man should possess private property.

It is true that he already possesses certain kinds of security, for example against illness, unemployment, and old age. We have already said that progress in these fields must be continued.

But security through solidarity does not solve the problem. Each individual likes to have the feeling of security that comes from having his own private possessions. The freedom to wait, to choose, to take a decision—these are strengthened if he possesses a "reserve" protecting him from outside uncertainties. This is both obvious and understandable.

Each person feels himself freer if he has possessions. The Frenchman's wish to own a house expresses the desire to be "master in his own house," that is to say, free. Owning a car meets the desire to move about where and when he chooses. Anyone who has traveled in collectivist countries will have observed that freedom flourishes only in the little plot of ground which peasants are allowed to keep around their house.

The principle that everyone has a right to property is found in every noncollectivist society. If only a few are allowed property, the law is making a basic distinction between the haves and the have-nots. Our democracy must ensure that all its members can acquire a minimum amount of private property.

This idea underlies the concept of participation put forward by General de Gaulle, and the plan for giving more people an opportunity of buying shares, which President Pompidou tried out. It also underlies housing policy over the past two years. In response to public opinion, preference has been given to house buyers. One Frenchman in two already owns his house or apartment.

We must go further still. We must recognize that the individual has a right to acquire property.

What is the nature of that right? Of course it does not mean that he must wait passively for society to give him property. It means that wages, the savings system, and credit facilities must be such that every person can be sure that in the course of a lifetime's work he can, if he wishes, obtain the money to acquire a minimum of private property.

This admittedly is an abstract right, but it can lead to the coherent organization of various institutions—building societies, profit-sharing, social and mutual credit schemes—adapted to various walks of life, and making possible the purchase of a house, of life insurance, or of stocks and shares.

This right should also lead to an effective system for preserving the real value of people's savings.

The amount of this minimum private property depends of course on the degree of development of the economy. It must grow as the economy grows and be periodically revised. It can serve as a point of reference in determining what proportion of an estate should be exempt from death duties and what contributions should be made toward an old-age pension.

More important, it enables the individual to find security and is therefore a kind of guarantee of his freedom.

A democratic society has the duty of applying its laws to all its members. Since France, with its rural origins and instincts, has always linked private property and freedom, it cannot apply that principle to some and not to others.

French democracy must recognize and establish the individual's right to acquire property within his society.

Part IV

━━━━━━━━━

THE
ORGANIZATION
OF POWER IN
FRENCH
DEMOCRACY

The pluralism of power guarantees freedom. Freedom must not be anarchy, any more than the diffusion of power must lead to impotence. Democratic progress does not end in disorder but in a higher balance of order within freedom and responsibility.

This is true of the running of the economy and social development; of the organization of collective life with the aim of preserving security and peace; and of the functioning of the state in a democratic society.

The organization of power in French society must make that society a well-ordered, strong, and peaceful democracy.

CHAPTER 8

The Management of the Economy and of Social Development

We still have much to accomplish if we are to ensure that society is really master of its economic progress. In a pluralist society this attempt to regulate the economy presupposes competition and a free market.

I ask the reader's indulgence for the difficult nature of the following pages. I have not introduced them out of pedantry nor, as can be imagined, to make the book lighter reading. I considered it necessary to treat this subject, for it lies at the heart of my argument, just as it lies at the heart of social life. The dryness of the text does not reflect a lack of interest in my subject matter, but rather a respect for it.

Competition and the free market are often viewed negatively by the French. They see in them a kind of disorganization or anarchy. A long-standing leaning toward statism, going back to Colbert and to the period of the Revolution and Empire, a tendency to prefer a senior civil servant to a company director, our Cartesian way of thinking, which results in a better understanding of mechanics than of biology, and finally the excesses and abuses committed in the name of liberty, explain this attitude of mind.

Such mistrust is justified to the extent that a democratic society, which has decided to make the spontaneous subservient to the conscious, cannot yield again to blind forces.

But a modern economy is an extraordinarily complex system, in which every day hundreds of thousands of items of information and decisions play a part. No collective centralization can make such a system work correctly. It can be run only with the help of powerful automatic mechanism.

Comparison with another complex system, the human body, will help us to understand. If each breath we draw, each step we take, had to be the result of a conscious decision, illness would soon follow. Basic functions such as breathing, looking, and walking are performed unconsciously, the brain being alerted only when something goes wrong. These automatic mechanisms do not diminish our mastery of our own body; they are rather the condition of that mastery, the brain being left free to give its whole attention to over-all control.

The analogy holds true of economics. If the production of such-and-such a wage or price had to be the result of a decision by society—what is called authoritarian planning—the result would be not increased mastery of economic activity, but simply a high degree of inefficiency and waste: in short, economic illness.

Theorists are trying in vain to modify such procedures, and wherever the procedures are in force this illness is found. It explains the slowing-down of growth as heavy industrialization is completed and the needs of a diversified economy appear.

* * *

This does not mean that our society must show no interest in the functioning of the economy. On the contrary, it must do everything in its power to place economic activity at the service of man.

It possesses the means. Public expenditure, which represents 40 per cent of national production and covers all fields of activity, taxes on the income and expenditure of individuals and companies, and stimulatory action on their investments, are powerful weapons in society's fight to gain control of its own development.

The use of these weapons must be based on careful consideration and on a middle and long-term view of the whole economy. Decisions should not be taken arbitrarily or unilaterally; they should be taken in the light of the views of all those responsible for economic and social life. Under these conditions a democratic society can consciously manage its own evolution. Such is the aim of French-style supple planning,* a transposition into economic terms of French democracy.

This kind of planning takes an over-all view of future development and it organizes consultations and meetings between those taking part in that development, so it is a good instrument for deciding democratically on a course of action.

Certainly much remains to be done in this field. The

---

* It has to be remembered that "planning," like many other words, has two very different meanings. *Authoritarian planning* is the power assumed by political authority to fix in detail levels of prices, wages, production, output, purchases, sales, investment, etc., and, should the occasion arise, to impose penalties for noncompliance. *Supple planning* is the action whereby, after full discussion with others concerned in the economy, the state *recommends* objectives to them and imposes *on itself* norms for the future.

creation of the central Council for Planning, which meets monthly in the house of the President of the Republic, in the presence of the Prime Minister, the Commissioner of the Plan, and Ministers with economic and social responsibilities, gives the government the means of better directing day-to-day action by the state toward long-term objectives. In this way it helps to put growth at the service of a democratic, over-all view of society.

If the choice of a course and the means toward attaining it are to be effective, the working of the economy requires the support of automatic mechanisms. This is a form of "power-assisted steering." The mechanisms are competition and market forces, which allow individual initiative and free enterprise to take basic decisions.

When compared with an economy based on authoritarian planning, even if it is termed democratic, a decentralized, regulated economy is a higher form of social organization, which allows the conscious mind to direct spontaneous movements.

This superiority is borne out by experience, for we know that economies run by authoritarian planning have mediocre levels of productivity and turn out poor-quality products, insufficiently adapted to consumer needs.

It is no mere coincidence that none of the countries with a high standard of living, countries we must constantly study in order to make ourselves one of them, practices authoritarian planning or intends to do so. Only an adept at that perverse form of dreaming called illusion would wish to head for such an impasse.

Even if it cares little about the details of economic mechanisms, the public must take note of the following two principles. They are complementary and form what Chinese thinkers would call a double unity. An advanced society cannot discharge the responsibility for running the economy onto competition and market forces alone; in order to run its own affairs consciously and efficiently, it must let the mechanisms of the market regulate the basic working of the economy, which it can then correct and complete. In this way the conscious mind picks up and guides spontaneous movements.

The day public opinion fully grasps these principles, France will have crossed the psychological barrier still separating it from the most advanced economies.

* * *

Run in this way, our economy will take as its first objective sustained employment and the mastery of inflation.

The objective of full employment is not unattainable, because it was achieved in France for twenty-five years running.

From 1950 to 1974, 5.3 million jobs were created in industry, business, and services. The total number of French men and women with nonagricultural jobs rose during this period from 13.8 million to 19.1 million, which proves the great capacity of an economy like ours to create jobs. Nevertheless, before the crisis came, there was a slow but continuous rise in the number of people seeking work for whom there were no openings.

A figure of 1 million people seeking work, 500,000 of them out of work for three months or more, with all the consequent privations and worry, is a major challenge for our society.

We should look further and ask whether we shall be able to maintain full employment once it returns. Or must our fellow citizens resign themselves to a high level of unemployment, an evil from which they believed themselves permanently sheltered?

One thing at any rate is certain: The solution to the

employment problem cannot be found in authoritarian planning of the economy.

Economies run by authoritarian planning usually leave their workers no choice about where they will live, what job they will do, what firm they will work for. The concept of full employment as we understand it has no meaning for them.

If the state had power to force unemployed persons to remain in country districts and so to disguise underemployment, France would not consider this the ending of unemployment. The very large number of people in collectivist economies who are so-called agricultural workers is an indication of the difficulties such economies have in creating enough jobs in industry, business, and administration.

Our demand for full employment is meaningful only in countries practicing freedom.

The lasting suppression of unemployment is, however, something which a pluralist economy like ours can achieve. During the worst of the recent crisis the level of unemployment in the Western economies reached only a third or a quarter of what it was during the great prewar crisis, thus validating the theories of Keynes and Beveridge, which taught us to fight underemployment by stimulating over-all demand and by investment.

We must go further than that. Permanent full employment is the overriding aim of an advanced economy, since it implies the full use of capacities and skills, while recognizing that man comes first in our society.

It involves a great number of different approaches. At the international level the industrial nations' conjunctural and monetary policies must be better co-ordinated. At home there must be better general and professional education of workers and future workers; the re-establishment, thanks to their revitalization, of discarded forms of employment; better use of land resources; elimination of many of the impediments to creating new jobs; progressive reduction of working hours and introduction of flexible hours. All these points have been tackled; progress has been made and must continue. It is important for us to realize that action such as the above is much more likely than an increase of bureaucracy to bring full employment, conceived as a dynamic balance.

* * *

Complementary to the goal of full employment, and indispensable to the progress of our society, is the fight against inflation.

Here too it would be an illusion to think that collectivism and authoritarian planning would produce better results.

Inflation is not absent from collectivist systems. Understood as the imbalance between goods offered and sought, it is rife. It is not apparent in prices, which are fixed by the state, but it takes the form of shortages. It can be measured now by the rise in the cost of living, now by the length of queues outside the shops. Sometimes the imbalance produces an explosion.

It is no coincidence that the currencies of the collectivist economies are not convertible, and valueless at an international level. They are not true money but coupons; they are not exchangeable for freely chosen goods and cannot be used in such a way as to retain their value. Hence, in international transactions, only currencies of free-enterprise countries are used.

In our type of economy it is not a scarcity of goods that chiefly causes inflation, but social groups competing fiercely for the "surplus" engendered each year by economic growth. It is most marked in countries where the conflict between social groups and their representative organizations is most intense; least marked in countries which, like Germany, have no price control but benefit from a will to collaborate on the part of all members of society, who believe that the existing economic and social system can be made better, even perfect.

From this we see how mistaken are those who claim that intensifying the class struggle would prevent prices rising. We see also what we have to do if our society is to beat inflation or at least keep it within acceptable bounds.

First of all, public opinion must fully understand the fundamental need to stabilize prices. Stable prices are an economic necessity, for inflation weakens our competitiveness and so directly threatens employment in an economy where two out of five workers produce for export. Stable prices are a social necessity, for inflation is unjust, even if many people have found ways of protecting themselves from it. Stable prices are also a national necessity, for beyond a certain level inflation shatters the social contract, leads to the breakdown of society, and places restrictions on an independent foreign policy.

Of course the state has a responsibility for fighting rising prices. Notably by budgetary and monetary means it must ensure basic economic equilibrium. It must also use all available methods, regulatory, administrative, and stimulatory, to fight abuses, to promote true competition, and to set an example of strictness.

But it would be a mistake to think that in a pluralist society the fight against inflation is only the state's business.

In such a society those engaged in the economy have a margin of initiative and freedom of action. This margin can be wider or narrower according to circumstances, but it must be substantial or society will fall into authoritarian planning and collectivism. In particular, free wage-bargaining and its corollary, the right to strike, are a fundamental element in the life of a pluralist society.

But freedom implies responsibility, in this case a responsible attitude by each of the partners in economic and social life, and indeed by every citizen, to keep prices and incomes at a moderate level. This is a basic fact of life in our society, which no one can challenge or escape. Here too the weight of public opinion must ensure that everyone is aware of the responsibility and does not shirk it. In this sphere it must provide ready, much-needed support for action by the state. That is what is called confidence, and it is also common sense.

But in my opinion the fight against inflation cannot be isolated from other areas of social progress in a democratic society.

An excess of inequalities engenders covetousness and resentment, and is therefore a powerful force behind inflation. The struggle against inequalities is one of the conditions of anti-inflationist policy.

Moreover, there is often an inhuman side to modern industrial and urban life, and this inevitably encourages the struggle for compensation, even if only apparent, by way of excessive wage raises. The steady improvement of the quality of life, the rebalancing of our human geography so that rural zones and small towns are developed, the increase in essential public services with the consequent improvement in the quality of life—all these are also long-term weapons against inflation.

Inflation reflects the tensions of social life and is a barometer of the difficulties a free society experiences in making balanced progress. So the lasting defeat of inflation will be a major objective of French democracy.

CHAPTER 9

The New Growth

In the coming years France's economic growth ought to continue at a still more vigorous rate. First because there are important individual and national needs still to be met; next because vigorous growth is a condition of full employment; lastly because if France is going to remain politically independent and influential both in Europe and in the world at large, we must become one of the leading industrial nations; in particular, by 1985 our industrial production ought to be comparable to West Germany's.

Every year in industry and agriculture, production methods and productivity ought to improve. Any economic policy that fails to take account of that is turning its back on France's interests.

But this growth, while continuing vigorous, must become a new growth. We must not be content with reproducing the same kind of growth and the same distribution of goods as in past years. Future growth must learn the lessons of events both before the crisis (the "gloominess" of a consumer society) and during the crisis (the need to economize on national resources), and must meet the needs of a new era. In this sense, it must be a new growth.

It will have four characteristics.

* * *

The new growth must be more equitable. As we have already said, if justice, solidarity, and greater national cohesion are to be achieved, we must see that more of the products of growth go to the weak and the dispossessed, in such a way as to eliminate poverty, end privilege, and reduce the inequalities that divide society. This policy must be pursued patiently and steadfastly by means of fiscal methods, social benefits, and wage policies.

* * *

The new growth must be better deployed, that is to say, better adapted to the new world markets, and to the special skills of the French economy—so as to make maximum use of our natural resources and the extra cachet of French workmanship.

In this area the distinctive qualities of a decentralized economy, especially its extreme flexibility, are trump cards. Contrary to a widely held view, industrial redeployment does not necessarily imply a particularly interventionist policy; above all it allows spontaneous adaptations to take place and sometimes facilitates them, and it refrains from providing artificial aids, however pressingly they are asked for, since these prevent adaptation.

Intervention may be necessary, but for other reasons. It may be necessary to graduate changes which impose too much strain on individuals, or to ease excessive difficulties. It may be necessary to shield the French economy from specialization which would make it too dependent on international suppliers or markets.

* * *

The new growth must be thriftier and gentler. During the past twenty-three years our sustained growth has been to the advantage of all, but it has been too costly in human and material terms.

These include monotonous, unhealthy, or unsafe working conditions, great inroads on natural resources, the rape of the environment, heavy and costly investments, and the upsetting of those balances within nature and within man's relations with nature which had persisted, miraculously unchanged, since earliest times.

Can that kind of growth be avoided? Today most people say yes, yielding to the easy temptation to redraw a course of events which at the time were desired and explicitly described as desirable. But it is true that the curve of unbridled growth, which broke down habits and protection systems, led to the exhaustion of natural resources and to neuroticism in society.

A decentralized economy must adapt itself to the needs of a growth which is civilized, and, shall we say, gentle. It has recourse to massive investment and massed concrete buildings only when no other solution is available; it is sparing of its resources and keeps human tensions to a minimum; it respects balances such as the balance of generations and social groups in towns, of activities in a region, of plant and human ecology.

A democratic state ought to promote gentle growth by providing information, recommending certain courses, and setting an example.

The President of the Republic should not be accused of petty meddling when he stops the building of a motorway opposite Notre Dame, when he puts a green space where the Halles used to be, when he protects the gardens of the Cité or has dark, anonymous tower blocks pulled down. He is trying to put forward the rudiments of a new social grammar, which will allow fuller expression of the needs and preferences of a population stifled by concrete, paper work, and a vicious circle of decisions, and unable to make its voice heard.

This policy can count on the support of various associations and ought also to be able to count on that of business firms, whose help can be useful in making gentle growth a reality of daily life.

* * *

Lastly, the new growth will be more useful, because better employed.

Everyone knows that the satisfaction people get from the resources procured by growth are not proportionate to those resources. Though it has been described as an instrument for the development of man and of human happiness, growth in fact loses a lot on the way and yields small dividends in terms of the quality of life.

To say this is not to condemn growth. I have stressed that growth is indispensable for us. It is rather an invitation to strive to improve its fruits.

As regards individual consumer goods, we have begun to take action. And action here is indispensable. The "consumer king" described in economics textbooks is rarely to be found in real life. A certain kind of advertising, the conditioning of products, their misleading diversification, and their built-in obsolescence are ways of manipulating the consumer and of falsifying consumer structures.

The collectivists propose to remedy this by even stricter planning. The remedy is probably as bad as the disease.

The consumer has been exposed to pressure by the producer. As in the fable of the oyster and the litigants, a third robber now appears, politics, which solves the problem to its own advantage; for the power to plan, whoever has it—be he a Minister, a civil servant, or an elected delegate—is a power to dispossess.

Collectivist thinkers' deep distrust of the individual, his initiative and his tastes, is well known. Hence their refusal to let him make choices. It is surely significant that no new consumer goods have been suggested or invented by a collectivist economy.

In a pluralist economy, on the other hand, it is the consumer who must be protected, so that he can choose freely. To ensure that advertisements do not make leading claims, to limit, if occasion requires, the too rapid introduction of new products or their apparent diversification: It is not the details of measures to be taken that matter here, but the intention, which is that the consumer's interests and preferences should be paramount.

Similar but even more difficult action must be taken with regard to the great social institutions: education, health, and town planning.

The smooth working of these great systems, of their equipment, and of the public services which run them, determines the quality of life for Frenchmen. That means that their improvement is a major objective.

Results already achieved allow us to envisage new approaches whereby quality will gradually become more important than quantity.

An in-depth analysis of the facts of social life is indispensable in order to clarify what action should be taken, and to distinguish between actual and assumed improvements. For example, if an increase in the number of old people's homes leads to the elderly leaving their own homes when they could have stayed there, that can hardly be called progress. Studying the conditions for a real improvement in the quality of life offers a vast field to the social sciences. Essential work can be done by local and regional institutions, which have a better knowledge of people's needs and are closer to actual conditions.

Progress can also be made in making more personal the services provided by the great social institutions, whether it be education, housing, health, transport, or leisure. This personalization, it is true, has limits both technical and financial. But it meets a social and political need; indeed, individual service to the public is a mark of a pluralist society.

In this spirit those who run the great public services should make a practice of soliciting the opinions of those who use them, for example, parents of schoolchildren, patients in hospital, and users of public transport.

Such people are not accustomed to speaking out. Sometimes they are kept silent or isolated by an administration that believes it alone knows what is in the public interest. Sometimes they are championed by organizations that are deemed to represent them but in fact use them for political ends, for battles which are not theirs.

All representatives of public services and social institutions have a fundamental obligation to try sincerely to collect the opinions of those they serve, to do so in conditions where underlying political motives and ideological sectarianism play as small a part as possible, and to attach the greatest importance to the opinions so expressed; and, better still, to allow customers to take part in the management of these services and systems.

The new growth will not be achieved in a day. But results to date indicate that in the course of the Seventh Plan there will be a marked upward swing.

* * *

Finally, long-term development raises the problem of a certain control of science. This problem confronts the whole human race, but especially the scientifically advanced countries.

The idea of controlling scientists' research offends our conception of science as the highest form of free and disinterested activity.

But such a move undoubtedly answers a social need. It is not aimed at those fundamental studies which increase our knowledge of the universe, of life, and of man. But the direction of applied research must be determined as a function of needs as seen by society. The cost of research and its possible consequences make this necessary.

The whole question has recently been raised on a world scale by the University of Paris. It should not be seen as a plan for limiting or truncating scientific development. I merely state that in a pluralist society desirous of controlling its own destiny a discussion should be started between scientists and representatives of the nation as a whole. Because it concerns us all it must not be restricted to the small world of offices and laboratories, but should take place openly.

CHAPTER 10

Freedom, Order, and Security

A society based on pluralism of power inevitably runs the risk of open defiance and disorder. Now disorder hands over the weak to domination by the strong and by those who make a lot of noise. And open defiance disintegrates society. Hence the need for order and security.

Order can be the result either of forcible restraint or of the peaceful use of freedom. Forcible restraint is the lot of most nations on our planet. Is it possible for us, who are free and disorderly, to attain peaceful order?

Contrary to a widely held opinion, this order cannot be the simple maintenance of order as it used to be. That was the order of a mainly rural society, where hardly any news circulated, where political philosophical and religious views, though freely expressed, left intact a universally recognized code of social behavior. A person in authority had only to appear wearing his insignia to make an impression and win respect.

That society and its kind of order have had their day. The immense majority of Frenchmen live in towns. Radio and television spread their excitable messages everywhere. Emancipation has spread to moral behavior also. Authority in itself has ceased to be an argument.

The new order which our society is seeking must take account of these facts. It cannot march booted and helmeted against the courage of history. It must be based on the practice of freedom. But is that realistic? The question is basic and the answer far from obvious, for history teems with examples of freedom degenerating into disorder and disorder rebounding into tyranny.

A liberal, democratic society will answer yes, and be ready to face the risks involved.

This optimism is justified and, I would add, fundamental. There is nothing shocking in the fact that in an open, free community men and women coexist while holding different views and different ways of life. There is no cause for alarm if what seemed obvious yesterday is questioned today. The right to be different is not equivalent to the right to be disorderly. On the contrary, no order can be deeply established or fully accepted if it does not respect this right to be different. Individual freedom in itself threatens no one.

But this optimistic choice must not lead to negligence or indifference. For man remains a curiously aggressive animal, always prone to violence. And violence, whether individual or collective, is something we cannot accept.

* * *

Public opinion has been shocked by acts of violence reported in the media. There have been attacks on the weak, on children and old people, and there have been muggings. People are worried by their frequency and they no longer feel safe when they go out at night. They probably do not realize that there are fewer acts of violence today than there were in the nineteenth century, which is generally considered an orderly age, but they are right in believing that violence has increased fast since 1965.

Society must take preventive action and impose sanctions. It cannot trust to miracles. Only preventive action will strike at the root of the evil. A group of distinguished specialists has therefore been asked to report on the origins of delinquency and crime. Police action, educational and leisure activities, have been stepped up in the suburbs and new towns, and adjusted to the new conditions.

Public opinion calls for sanctions. These can dissuade people from crime, but they also raise the fundamental question of the death penalty, which no society can shirk. My job is to respect the laws, not to express my personal belief. But one point must be made quite clear. The right to pardon is not the same as passing judgment or even deciding on a punishment. Those are the sovereign rights of the courts, and of the citizens appointed as jurors. The right to pardon is the right to mitigate a sentence, in exceptional cases and on humanitarian grounds.

To begin a debate on the death penalty at the present time would mean raising the dread conflict between fear and life, between horror at the crime and horror at the punishment. For that reason the only positive course of action, although it is a painful one, is, initially, to increase preventive and security measures, while awaiting the moment when society, freed from fear, can debate fully man's mysterious, sometimes terrible, but unalterable right to life.

* * *

Collective violence raises problems of a different kind for our democracy.

Social violence wears many guises. It makes its appearance long before it takes the form of physical disorder. As soon as a force, a power, or a group, driven by self-interest or passion, begins to overstep the limits without respect for the common good, it introduces violence into society.

This holds true of industry. It is normal for industry to try to produce wealth, for that is its job. But if it does so without regard to the safety or working conditions of its employees, of the good faith of its customers, or of the natural environment, in short of the social interests blocking its way to profit, it is guilty of social violence, of what its victims consider an act of aggression.

That is also true of mass organizations of any kind. Nothing is more natural than that they should defend the interests of their members. But if they systematically make demands known to be unacceptable to the other party, if they seek not compromise but the other party's defeat or a complete break, if, in order to make their power felt, they take advantage of the fragile, complex structures, driven by a delicate system of balances, which comprise modern society, then they are committing an act of social violence.

The same holds true when civil servants, drawing strength from the administration's prerogatives, refuse to listen to someone explaining a difficult case, or, declining to treat that person as a human being, take the easy way out by applying a rule which they know to be unsuitable.

It is true lastly of the mass means of communication, written or audio-visual. When they transmit news, even hard-hitting news, when they show pictures of real life, even startling or cruel ones, when they accompany the pictures with a deeply felt commentary, they are doing their job. But when, in the name of their duty as reporters and sheltering behind the right of self-expression, they carry the taste for sensationalism to the point of grossly oversimplifying the facts; when this leads to a self-satisfied display of attitudes or manifestations of collective violence, or to the systematic dramatization of insignificant, quickly forgotten events, the public once again finds itself faced with a kind of aggression.

It is a fact that in a democracy there are various forms

of behavior which cannot be curbed by law but which introduce a degree of violence.

No doubt we could adopt an attitude of resignation and view them as a by-product of freedom.

But violence is like a sandstorm on a statue: It erodes, disfigures, and finally engulfs it. He who sows the wind reaps the whirlwind. Peace and tolerance are necessary to France's pluralist democracy.

Where are they to come from?

* * *

They can be expected only from people themselves as they play their various roles in society, and from those at the center of power, including of course the state, provided that they make an effort to reflect on their task and take account of public opinion.

A democratic society has a right to expect from them moderate and responsible behavior.

It is for them to preserve the freedoms they enjoy, and to avoid sapping them by violent behavior. Business firms and groups with common economic interests, representative organizations and pressure groups, and the media too, must seriously ponder the question: How far do I have the right to go?

The problem is particularly difficult for mass organization and the mass media. The rights at stake—the right of banding together, the right to self-expression—are so fundamental that any setting-up of boundaries, any restriction, is repugnant to the people of a democracy, who do not see how they can proceed in that direction without preventing the exercise of those freedoms.

So they are virtually unorganized, in France as in most other democracies. That is an odd situation when one stops to think about it, since we are dealing with the kind of power which can lock society's delicate machinery, and erupt into millions of homes. It is the individual who suffers: Libels, false news, impeding the right to work, to give only a few examples, are almost never dealt with by the courts. As for the public generally, it is a long established fact that they are the chief victims of abuses committed in the name of freedom.

We find that freedom to do business, to form an organization, to express an opinion, has a different nature depending on whether it is exercised individually or collectively. The individual's right to freedom is inherent in democracy and his exercise of that right never endangers democracy. On the other hand, the collective exercise of freedom, which amounts to a "power"—a counter-power or anti-power—lies halfway between freedom and power.

The only moderation possible is self-discipline. It is true that the power of the state can oppose the worst excesses. But the state is obliged to remain prudent, in order not to strike down freedom in the course of attacking power, like the Greek warrior under the walls of Troy who was afraid to throw his spear at his enemy for fear of wounding the goddess Athena.

That is why democratic society must be able to count on the self-discipline of its members. It must urge all those who exercise collective freedom to reflect publicly on the rules they should themselves draw up: objectivity, moderation, respect for others' feelings, the duty to correct false information. In a pluralist society not only the lawgiver at the center but each social group should lay down limits which must not be crossed, because crossing them would increase violence.

Both the impetus and the sanctions lie with public opinion. Public opinion decides where freedom stops and disorder begins. Its decrees are sovereign. It is fundamental that public opinion should unambiguously support moderation and responsibility against irresponsibility and violence.

To do this we must not wait for physical disorder to erupt. Political opinions have no place here, and the violence of friends is no more to be condoned than that of opponents.

In a democratic society opinion must show no mercy for violence, that is to say, for excess, outrage, and extremism, for selfishness that is indifferent to solidarity, for politics based on the worst in human nature.

A democratic society must train itself to have a reflex action of repulsion for faces flushed with fury and near-hysterical voices, and for the language of excess and threats. It must denounce them whenever and from whatever quarter they appear.

In this way democratic society will defend its own freedom and ensure that it continues to exist in peace.

CHAPTER 11

A Strong and Peaceful Democracy

There can be no freedom and no order without organized representative political institutions.

Since the time of Marx, it is true, many in Western society have believed the opposite. In a society completely free of injustice and estrangement, the state will become useless. It will wither away. A society of citizens will find in itself both peace and order, and will have no need of a political power to maintain them.

It is one of history's ironies that in the name of this optimistic theory, and to prepare the way for a stateless society, one of the most concentrated forms of power known to man has been established on a large part of the earth's surface.

To acknowledge that does not, however, solve the problem. For there exist utopias which, even when contradicted by the facts, remain prophetic.

That is not the case here. The concept of human nature on which this doctrine is based is contradicted by all that we learn from the scientific study of man, recent though such study is. He is not an innocent, peaceful being, a food-gatherer crowned with flowers, whose fraternal relations have been misdirected by a perverted society. He is capable of the best, but also of the worst, when the triple fires of desire, hate, and ignorance flare up in him. And he is capable of not seeking possessions and power. We should remember that our animal brothers have societies that are strictly hierarchical, and they defend their patch of territory tooth and claw.

Political institutions are necessary to the pluralist society. Curtailing the role of the state would not bring about an end to power; it would simply place power in private hands. Only public power protects us from the excess of private power.

* * *

That fact should not lead us to deify the state.

The state is only an instrument for serving the nation. France's substance lies in its people and in its soil. The state must be conceived, administered, and perfected with a view to the service it can render to both.

A pluralist society must possess an authentically democratic state. That means that its governmental organs receive their powers from free elections, held at regular intervals. It means also that there is a freely formed opposition, expressing itself without check and able to canvass votes with the same rights as the majority party, so long as it respects the laws binding on the country's institutions.

Pluralist democracy is, by nature, dialectic. Only the existence of an opposition, the criticisms it makes, and the alternative that it embodies give real power to the sovereignty of the citizen. He becomes an arbiter, the person who has the casting vote and to whom final appeal is made.

It is very easy to discover whether a political regime is democratic or not, at least in industrialized countries, for developing countries present different problems. It is useless to listen to what those who run the country say. Does the regime allow the existence of an effective opposition, genuinely able to take its place as a majority party? Then it is truly democratic and popular. If it refuses to allow such an opposition, then whatever the explanations offered, it is neither popular nor democratic.

In administering the pluralist society, the state must not encroach, nor must it be arbitrary.

A society where the powers are separated and where individuals have responsibility is the opposite of a bureaucratic society.

The state cannot of course be restricted to the functions it had under the monarchy: defense, justice, and finance. All the important social tasks, such as education, health, environment, industrial and agricultural development, in one form or another require some degree of state intervention or participation. Consequently it is useless to define in advance all the functions of the state or to try to put some sort of theoretical limit on its intervention.

But it must be understood that a nonbureaucratic state aims at helping the pluralist society to face up to its responsibilities, not to replace that society. It intervenes only if private action, whether interested or disinterested, prove powerless to accomplish a social or economic task deemed indispensable.

Similarly, it prefers to intervene temporarily, to put a situation right or to repair machinery, rather than to intervene permanently. For direct intervention, which increases the state's sphere of influence, it substitutes indirect intervention, by way of agreements, contracts, recommendations, and incentives.

The pluralist state does not bake bread, on the grounds that people need bread, nor practice medicine, on the grounds that citizens should be healthy. It respects the legitimacy and utility of private enterprise. It wants to serve a society of men, not to lie in wait to devour that society.

The pluralist state is not an arbitrary power.

The state has accomplished great things in France, but it has left behind bad memories as well as good, and thereby aroused an instinctive, lasting distrust. We have had the state of the old regime, capricious and enjoying too many privileges; the authoritarian, bloodstained state of the end of the Revolution and the Empire; the cold, cruelly indifferent state of the bourgeois monarchy and bourgeois Republic; the flabby, shameless state of the period between the wars.

To protect themselves from the state, the French have gradually subordinated its power to respect for the law. That task is still not fully complete. The legislature has recently been made subject to more active control by the Constitutional Council. And the Council of State, which reviews the executive power from lowest to highest level, must be given the powers it needs to ensure that its decrees are carried out whatever the circumstances.

It is essential for the state to obey the letter of the law. But that is not enough. In a pluralist democracy it must work hard to find out, and to respect, the citizens' interests and opinions.

This does not mean that it must come round to their opinion in every instance, or that it can ever disregard the interests of this or that individual or group. But it does mean that its responsibilities are such that it may not act without consultation, take a decision without explaining why, or break off discussions without having done what is necessary to come to an agreement.

These modern rules, based on prior explanation, consultation, and concerted measures, are a sign not of weakness, but of respect for the pluralist society.

They are, we well know, still imperfectly applied. They demand from representatives of the executive power —from the Minister, the head of department, and each civil servant—an effort that seldom comes naturally. They presuppose a genuine modesty, that is to say an awareness that a degree or high office does not make a man omniscient; a real respect for the citizen; the realization that "the man in the street" has something to say about his own case and is a good judge of his interests; a gift for listening and talking, despite the language barriers in our complex modern society; the dropping of pretentious, useless, specialist jargon; the courage to discuss directly with individuals and groups: in short, a state of mind at the opposite pole from the technocratic-bureaucratic mentality to which large organizations inevitably give rise.

As well as respecting rights and avoiding arbitrary decisions, the pluralist state must be strong.

It must be strong not only to make the French community respected abroad, but at home to prevent groups of interests and mass organizations from overreaching their legitimate functions in society and becoming feudal states within the state; from turning their power to their own profit; from imposing their aims or opinions to the detriment of the common good.

A strong power must be independent.

A small minority in the opposition makes the unlikely charge that the government embodies "the power of monopolies," that is, of big business. In its way this slogan appears to express the need people feel for the state to be independent. It is quite true that a state in the service of certain big firms would be betraying its most important duty.

But must we accept the slogan which the same minority uses to define its ideal of government: "the power of the workers"?

The phrase is felicitous, but only at first sight. For man is not just a worker. He is also a consumer, a user, a saver. He has a family and a private life. Why shouldn't those aspects of his personality, those social functions, have a right to expression? Besides, when our countrymen are questioned about their worries today, they put fear of inflation at the top of the list; and that is the reaction of a consumer rather than of a worker. And old people, women without any training, young people being educated or trained—are they second-class citizens? The "power of the workers" demanded by the slogan means in fact the power of such-and-such an organization using the workers' name. It is only another way of saying: Power for us!

The pluralist state's slogan is: Power for the citizens. That is to say, for men and women, in all their diversity and complexity, in their right to be different, and in their fundamental equality.

As well as being independent, the state must know how to make itself respected.

Not because it is spelled with a capital letter, not in order to revive the high priesthood of the Pharaohs, not in order to help a caste or class to maintain its privileges or impose its views, but because, without a democratic state that is respected, no community can function freely.

Respect is no longer something given; it is won. The toga, the judge's red robes, the kepi, no longer suffice to establish it.

Growth of a critical spirit is a form of progress, but on condition that it does not turn into denigration and negativism. Those who exercise authority have an obligation to win respect for authority by making decisions that are just, and by their general behavior.

* * *

Political institutions must ensure the stability and efficiency indispensable to democratic life.

The Constitution adopted by the French people in 1958 has made possible a better balance between the public powers and ensured a stable executive. In his right to dissolve Parliament the President of the Republic possesses a prerogative which counterbalances the power of Parliament to bring down the Government. Conversely, Parliament can censure the Government only by carrying a motion with an absolute majority. The Government, appointed by the President of the Republic, is thereby better protected from maneuvering by individuals and parties. For that reason these rules must be scrupulously applied and respected.

The reform of 1962 laid down that the President of the Republic should be elected by universal suffrage, thus making his power depend on the people's vote. He receives his authority from them, and to them, inevitably, he will have to render account.

It would seem indispensable that the Government should be united in strength behind the policy they are pursuing, for the French, who are by tradition critical of the authorities, decline to be governed by men who disagree among themselves. On the other hand, we must not be surprised if some of the proposals laid before Parliament by the Government sometimes give rise to difficult discussions.

A pluralist democracy is not an acquiescent democracy. Once the executive is sure of being in office for a definite term, it is in the nature of our institutions that it should persuade Parliament that its plans are sound and strive to obtain Parliament's approval for them.

If its primary task is to exercise control over the executive, Parliament is also an arena for political activity between one general election and the next. There the important debates should take place. There the reforms necessary to the progress of social life should be thoroughly discussed.

We have a historic opportunity in possessing institutions which are both efficient and democratic. But they are fairly recent, and therefore still subject to question, all the more so since some people pay them only lip service.

Everything must be done to preserve them.

The real trouble with politics in France is not the nature of its institutions, but the fact that political debate is unnecessarily dramatic.

Democratic life, it is true, consists of debate and of competition between politicians and parties. But these can take place in two ways. Either they presuppose basic agreement about certain principles of social life, or they pit one view of society against a wholly opposed view.

In the democracies that work most smoothly—in the United States, Great Britain, West Germany, and northern Europe—we find the former situation. It is true that elections seem to divide those countries into two equal parts; that is usual when a new government has to obtain a majority of popular votes. But they do not feel themselves cut in two, because the chief political parties share the same view of the organization of society. Their differences take place within that framework. Each of the contending parties realizes that the others intend to preserve essentials.

Their rivalry is not a war but a competition. The fact that they alternate in power produces not a series of chaotic upheavals, heralded as dramas and feared as revolutions, but a series of curves in the progress of society. The countries I have mentioned entrust government now to one party, now to another, but both share the same basic philosophy; in this way they harmonize the needs of continuity with those of change.

To alternate is in the nature of advanced democratic societies, and their pluralist organization is not questioned by any of the main groups which compose such societies. That is the way peaceful democracies regulate their political life.

Alone among advanced democracies, France is characterized by ideological divorce, and today this prevents us enjoying the kind of harmony I have described. Everything takes place as though political debate was not a race between two competing tendencies but the clash of two mutually exclusive truths. The mood is not that of citizens discussing their affairs, but rather that of a religious war barely tempered by the fact that the protagonists live side by side.

This state of affairs originates in our temperament and our history. Our political life has always been heightened by Mediterranean passion and a Latin liking for absolutes. Voltaire's call to banish intolerance is a cry in the wilderness.

Today there is no good reason for such a situation. France, we have seen, is not a country divided into two opposed social classes, but a society already well on the way to being unified. Our political parties do not correspond to social groups. Our political divisions arise less from unavoidable sociological factors, as is sometimes claimed, than from historical traditions and the temperament of the individual.

The direction in which we must look for progress in our political life now becomes evident.

First, we must carefully preserve the democratic institutions we have already achieved: their fundamental political and institutional rules, political neutrality in such spheres as the judiciary, the army, schools, and the civil service. To bring political strife, with its intolerance and exclusions, into these essential institutions, would not be democratic progress, as some people claim, but a dangerous regression. Any attempt to do this must be resisted.

We must also resist the attempt to make political rivalry a sort of civil war, fought with new kinds of weapons. If our democracy is to be modernized, the nervous tension must be taken out of French political life.

By dramatizing our political life and hardening our attitudes we play into the hands of those who oppose pluralism. By emphasizing that what divides France is stronger than what unites it, they seek to justify the excesses and the injustice of their attacks. Conversely, any attempt to stress that Frenchmen must learn to live together and respect one another's opinions prepares people's minds for democratic pluralism.

Every sincere believer in pluralism has a historic task: to make irreversible the French people's choice of a pluralist structure of power and society. On their determination and persuasiveness depend our chances of strengthening the institutions of the Fifth Republic and of once and for all committing our country to modern democracy. For that reason we call on a majority of the French people to join together, as in the early days of the Fifth Republic, in order to ensure the success of that decisive choice.

Then the real political debate will begin, here as among our neighbors, within a concept of society accepted by the great majority of Frenchmen, a tolerant society, openly respecting the separation of powers and the right to different opinions: a pluralist society.

The debate will not be a mythical battle with the Gorgons, the kind of battle between good and evil which still stains our political life with primitive, dangerous violence, but a competition in which men, and singly or in groups, can work in turn for the common good.

France will then have a strong and peaceful democracy.

CHAPTER 12

French Democracy in the World

I remember visiting, some years ago, the mill of Valmy, east of Rheims. Behind its gray wooden structure you see the plains, divided by hedges, where the young Revolutionary army, wearing blue uniforms with red facings, and clogs, defeated the armies of Europe's coalition. They were faced with professional soldiers and they won because of their burning patriotism.

Last October I crossed the plain where the Battle of Borodino was fought. It is a striking battlefield because there is hardly any cover, and such a short distance separated the mound where Napoleon stood and the famous Russian redoubt, barely nine feet high, which the French took by storm in the evening, in a welter of bodies, cannon, and horses. What force drove those men to fight, two thousand miles from the plains of Beauce and the copses of Poitou, if it was not burning patriotism?

That same patriotism we have seen more recently and painfully at Verdun and in the ashes of Auschwitz.

France is bound to her children by a strong and lasting tie, which a democratic society must preserve and make even stronger. This tie is the respect and attachment Frenchmen feel for France.

So the democratic society will not be satisfied with solving Frenchmen's problems, while neglecting France's. It must establish France's position in the world more firmly and lastingly. Its foreign policy will be based on the will to remain independent and the practice of solidarity and co-operation.

* * *

Is independence a realistic attitude for a nation not a superpower, living in a world knitted together by thousands of close relationships, where ideas and people are continually on the move?

Everyone knows that independence can no longer mean isolation and self-sufficiency. But do we have to accept domination by the superpowers as something inevitable? Our own and other nations' histories, as well as contemporary events, show us how much strength and reserve power lies in the will to be oneself. This strength is akin to the strength we have been looking at in this book: men's determination to govern themselves.

We see now what the will to remain independent means. It means the right to decide for ourselves, in the last resort, everything we consider essential for the French nation.

But such a right is not something given; it has to be won. It presupposes that France can count on its own armed forces in order to ensure its safety, that France will continue, as in the past eighteen years, to follow a defense policy commensurate with its position and its dangers. That policy is centered on the nuclear deterrent. It is comforting to find that after having been violently criticized by the Opposition, which tried to organize the French people against it, this crucial decision seems now to have won general approval. That is just reward for the man who thought out the policy and defended it for so long. In the same way Frenchmen must understand that, even though the cost be high, it is vital for them to have the conventional forces necessary to meet a variety of situations, and to maintain France's status in Europe.

But independence is more than a matter of defense forces. By refusing to borrow too heavily abroad, by continuing the search for adequate sources of energy, by keeping technological research and performance at a high level, we are also strengthening our independence. In the long-term view, independence justifies continued effort in those fields.

Independence, finally, is the reward of unity.

Many times in their history, as though they took a secret pleasure in it, Frenchmen have rended one another. France has then become vulnerable to others' greed and strength. But whenever they have been able to preserve their unity, or rediscover it, Frenchmen have been able to defend their country's independence. It is a long lesson, written in a thousand years of history, which must be kept constantly in mind.

*　*　*

In the world today independence naturally goes hand in hand with solidarity and co-operation.

Europe is being organized all around us. France has made a positive contribution to Europe by being one of the first to sign the Treaty of Rome, by the healing of relations with Germany—the work of General de Gaulle and Chancellor Adenauer—and, more recently, by the setting up of a Council of Europe.

Our country considers it essential that the nations of Western Europe, which are much alike in their way of life, civilization, and political institutions, should unite in a world where superpowers are emerging and where other groups of states are already banding together: oil producers, nonaligned countries, members of the Organization of African Unity.

French democracy has clear ideas about the union of Europe. We shall not try to impose a detailed plan on others, but we intend to prevent Europe dissolving into confused or impotent structures.

First of all economic and monetary union must be completed, according to the terms of the Treaty of Rome. It has to be admitted that this much-needed union is still a long way off. Our number one task is to make it a reality.

Next we must make progress with the confederal machinery of the European Union.

This is a difficult task, and a new one, which calls for drive, imagination, and pragmatism by all the Union's partners. And it is indispensable if Europe is to take its place in the groupings that will decide the destiny of the world. As for the necessary steps to that end, they must be decided by national governments and parliaments, the only institutions able to organize the confederal union of Europe.

The completion of economic and monetary union and the realization of European Confederation—these are France's inner bastion of solidarity.

Democratic France will join in developing an outer bastion of international co-operation.

France no longer regards diplomacy in terms of conflicts. We no longer make territorial claims and other countries do not make territorial claims on us. We do not practice imperialism, economic, cultural, or, of course, political.

It is true that the world is still dominated by a balance of force between the superpowers and the nations belonging to the main alliances. The clash of ideologies leads here and there to intervention. As long as this situation lasts France will continue to exercise its responsibilities with vigilance, honoring her alliances, working for peace, and respecting people's right to self-determination.

France will continue to work patiently for détente. If it does not solve every problem, at least détente is the only road leading to greater peace. Economic and technical cooperation, cultural relations, regular summit meetings of heads of governments, make it possible for states with different systems to share information and ideas, thus facilitating the solution of particular problems. France is pleased with the state of mind of its chief partners in détente. It would like détente to become still more of a reality through bilateral action and through moderation in ideological confrontation.

Beyond alliances and détente lies the huge area stretching to the ends of the earth, where France co-operates with other countries.

We co-operate, first, with those countries that share our culture and to which we are bound by ties of mutual affection. I am thinking of the independent states of Africa, whose dignity and independence we respect, and with whom we have established a remarkable degree of understanding. France will continue to give them financial and other help to preserve their dignity and independence, which both we and they consider an example to the world.

France co-operates also in solving problems that concern all nations. The international economy is still reeling under the blow of the 1973 crisis. Instead of yielding to the temptation and dangers of confrontation, France has decided to take part in discussions. These are thorny and beset by difficulties. Our decision was not dictated by circumstance. It expressed our lasting conviction that the solution of major problems concerning the world's economic development and security can be found no longer in a purely national or even regional framework, but only at world level.

* * *

To assert its independence France does not need to be cantankerous. And when it practices co-operation France does not risk being diminished, for it has a vocation to co-operate.

A country of world ideas, scene of the greatest political revolution of modern times, possessed of a language and culture which have spread far and wide, democratic France will not retire within itself. It will remain an inventive partner, respected by the modern world; preserving its personality intact, but opening its mind and heart to the great changes of our time and the new solidarity which today binds mankind together.

Conclusion

AN AMBITION
FOR FRANCE

I wonder how the reader would describe the plan outlined in the book he has just read.

It lies at the opposite pole from collectivism. The nature of a collective system, which crushes and denies the individual, runs counter to French aspirations.

Nor is it a plan for classical liberalism, such as America conceived and still practices. Not that we underrate the simple strength of the liberal view. But on the individual at the center of the system, face to face with all the dangers of life and all the encroachments of his fellow men, it often lays too heavy a burden, too unjust a way of life, and a loneliness that can border on despair.

The plan we have put forward has affinities with the future model of society in Europe. The model does not have a name but we see it taking shape, with variations from country to country, throughout this precious stretch of land on the edge of Asia where a certain conception of man, of his capacities and the power of his reason, began its long journey across the world.

Is it a "capitalist" plan? Obviously not, because it is based on the idea of pluralism, and in cases where arbitration is necessary it entrusts this not to capital but to the democratic expression of the people's sovereignty.

Is it opposed to socialism? In this book the words "socialism" and "socialist" have been purposely avoided. We speak of the socialism of West Germany, the socialism of Eastern Europe, the socialism of developing countries; a word applied to such different systems cannot be used without ambiguity.

If socialism means a sense of solidarity, and the will that society should be organized in such a way that it can choose the direction in which it will progress, there is nothing there that contradicts what we have just said. But if it means manipulation of the masses, initiative and responsibility paralyzed by a central bureaucracy, and an economy disorganized by irresponsible experiments or cut off from the rest of the world, then, it is true, it completely contradicts our plan.

What we propose is a modern democratic society, liberal in the sense that all its powers are organized in a pluralist structure, progressive by virtue of its good economic performance, its social unification, and its cultural achievements. It represents our ambition for France.

* * *

In describing that society, I am thinking less of a plentiful supply of material goods than of what lies beyond.

I can hear protests. It is true that we need a new rise in national wealth in order to end poverty altogether, to get more social justice, to improve the quality of life, and, despite its limited area and population, to keep our country a first-rate power.

This new step forward is indispensable. But the new horizon we increasingly feel the need of lies beyond, in the search for another dimension, suited to our times.

An exclusively materialist concept of society shuts man up within his desires and appetites and leaves him hungry and thirsty, even though his wants are filled. He then begins to notice a glimmer of a different sort of light. There have recently been signs of this in widespread condemnation of the consumer society and a craze for zero growth. Perhaps such attitudes went too far, but they show that people are groping for a new dimension of social life, one that gives expression to the life of all mankind.

That light must not go out.

The new dimension of social life which our age is seeking will more and more take the form of solidarity and fraternity.

The field for fraternal action is obviously more or less restricted. For many of us it is confined to the narrow but important circle of private life. For others, let us hope, there is a wider field of action and an opportunity of removing the unsmiling masks which industrial life has clamped to our faces. And why should that awareness of brotherhood not extend to our neighbors in Europe, and to the impoverished, suffering peoples of the world? Why shouldn't it reach out progressively to every member of the human race?

* * *

As we build our pluralist society, revolution becomes pointless; but on the other hand, we cannot remain static.

We must reform. Society must find the energy it needs to improve what must be improved, the maturity to debate essential questions, the patience to put reforms in hand, and the perseverance to complete them. We need a lion's strength and a fox's patience.

The responsibility for directing this task lies with those who hold political power. But they need support from the main social groups.

They need the support of executives, specialists, and managers. A pluralist society does not possess a backbone in the form of a single party or totalitarian organization. It rests on the skill and responsibility of those men and women who, at every level, are fortunate enough to be highly trained and in a position to make decisions.

The pluralist democracy needs the support of all workers, who, it should be recognized, have an essential role to play and for whom suitable opportunities must be ensured within a unified society.

The pluralist democracy needs the co-operation of scientists and intellectuals, because their research and sense of responsibility filter down to society as a whole. The pluralist democracy is not a predetermined society, but one in course of being created, and it needs everyone's ideas and help.

Lastly, this society needs the support of young people, and is intended for them. It is up to young people to argue about it, change it, and make it their own.

* * *

Some will say that the whole plan is too complex. True, it cannot be wrapped up in a slogan, but is that a criticism or a compliment?

We cannot desire a wide range of freedoms and responsibilities, we cannot prefer autonomy in our local life and in business, we cannot allow each person an area of privacy, and at the same time opt for a single, centralized, simplified system.

Just as the economy is becoming increasingly complex, so society's decisions, institutions, and responsibilities will become diversified.

Something within us is always calling for simplification, even for oversimplification. But that is a primitive instinct, like violence, and not very different from ignorance.

A society of freedoms will be an evolved society, perhaps less easy to describe than preregulated societies, but more elaborate, more knowledgeable, and, in a word, superior.

We have learned to accept things which used to be incomprehensible: the transmission of pictures over huge distances, the understanding of statistical data. One day we will come to accept as a fact the diversity and unity of a society of freedoms. It is worthy of note that such a society was foreseen by the earliest prophets of socialism as a final stage in society's growth. Often the means they proposed did not lead there. But at least they recognized its attractions and superiority.

* * *

Europe is uniting. And France is a part of Europe which must not be overshadowed: France has come so far, the France of battlefields and revolutions, of shouting in the streets and calm mornings in the countryside; now France can tear itself to pieces, as so often in the past, or become suddenly alert and thoughtful, and be one of the first nations to cross the threshold of a new organization of society.

For that France requires a plan which calms disputes instead of fomenting them. A plan that can be worked out in freedom and justice, a plan that respects differences of opinion in the long march toward unity.

Hence this plan, conceived for France.

* * *

After our efforts in common have opened new paths and liberated and humanized society, we must wait for some individual, or more likely a movement by the collective consciousness, to emit the beam of light needed to illuminate the world, the light of a new civilization that takes a spiritual view of man's liberation and of the future course of the human race.

As yet, we do not know what that course will be.

September 7, 1976